OUT OF STEP
by
Seán Kenny

Published by Hejukian Press
Dublin, London & San Francisco

Contact: seanzerocarbon@gmail.com

Novels by Seán Kenny:

The Hungry Earth
Fast-Wing
Celtic Fury
The Memory Trap
The Ulstermen
The King Snake

*For my parents,
Doreen and Johnny*

Author's Note

This is a memoir, not an autobiography. It tells the true story of a specific aspect of my life. I say this here to head off the inevitable whataboutisms of all the other peccadillos and transgressions that go unmentioned. And yes, I could fill another volume with those. But to what end? Many of the best known memoirs, excluding the inevitable effluence of celebrity potboilers, are coming of age stories. Mary Karr's *The Liar's Club*, Frank McCourt's *Angela's Ashes*, and Augustin Burrough's *Running With Scissors* tell of a child overcoming hideous circumstances on the way to productive adulthood. They are composed of a sequence of unrelated episodes that nevertheless lead to a specific uplifting conclusion.

Out Of Step hews closer to classic fiction. The first and last pages are connected, not just by stand-alone episodes, but by events that lead from one to the next. A million wasted lives is just human history but one wasted life is a human tragedy, to paraphrase Stalin. My life to this point was certainly not wasted, it was at worst misled, but it would certainly have been neglectful to shun this story, which only revealed itself in the last few years. Michelangelo famously remarked that the statue was already within the Carrara marble and he need only take hammer and chisel to it to reveal David or Bacchus. With the last missing link in my grasp I had only to take notebook and laptop to the events of my life to lay bare how one choice inevitably led to the next over almost the last half century.

Writing a memoir that seeks to shed light on old family injustices is a recipe for conflict by which I mean conflict outside the confines of the pages. It would hardly be worth the writing or the reading if it did not lead to a satisfying ending, meaning a denouement that makes sense of all that led up to it but remained hidden from the reader until they read those last pages. And it would still be hidden were it not for a chance remark on a random phone call in the summer of twenty twenty-two. Then, slowly but surely, the sun shone into one place in my head after another, the mists evaporated, and what long lay in darkness came into the light.

So will I turn her virtue into pitch,
And out of her own goodness make the net
That shall enmesh them all.

Iago

Othello, *Act II, Scene 3, lines 351-353*
by
William Shakespeare

Prologue. 1928 - 2001

My father was born to my then teenage grandmother in nineteen twenty-eight. Had my grandfather, ten years older, a mechanic in the Irish Air Corps, not quietly married her she would almost certainly have ended up in a Magdalene laundry and the nuns would have sold my father to some wealthy American. Instead he became the oldest of five children to a hero of the Irish war of independence. They lived in the village of Clondalkin to be close to Baldonnel aerodrome where Ireland's tiny air force was based. In his childhood years he lived in a house with an outside toilet but over time my grandfather rose through the ranks of the civil service and they bought a new semi-detached house a few hundred yards away with a proper bathroom, a cast iron range and a tiny wall-mounted fridge in the kitchen and three upstairs bedrooms.

The village boasted a Carmelite monastery, a Tudor castle, and a Round Tower which was all that remained of what had once been a flourishing monastic settlement on the banks of the fast-flowing Camac river. Founded in the seventh century it was an easy day's march from Dublin Bay and plundered by the first waves of Vikings. The only evidence of it known to have survived is a single illuminated manuscript which is held in a museum in Germany. Since Clondalkin lies half-way between Dublin and The Pale it is a fair bet that Tully's Castle held an English garrison that could sally forth to intercept any would-be mere Irish cattle raiders. The castle fell into ruin, but the Round Tower, rising ninety feet into the air with its conical stone roof, has never leaked in the thousand plus years since Saint Cronan's bell first peeled out across the meadows.

The monastery was built in the early nineteenth century and this was where my father went to school, followed by his three younger brothers. He was a studious child and went on to secondary school at Synge Street Christian Brothers, a six mile bike ride away in Dublin City. He played Gaelic games and became a fluent Irish speaker, spending at least one summer in Donegal, Ireland's remote north-west county. He would have traveled there on three different steam trains. He applied for a scholarship to University College Dublin, was accepted and graduated with a degree in engineering.

This was unprecedented and from then on a framed photo of my father in his mortar and gown, clutching his rolled up degree, with his own father standing next to him, took pride of place on the sideboard in MotherKenny's sitting room. He worked briefly for a couple of government agencies, and then, the icing on the cake, the piece de resistance, he became an officer in the Irish army. What this did for the status of the Kenny family cannot be overstated. Dad would often use the phrase "officer caste" when I was growing up. It was a British army term derived from the Hindu caste system in India. The lower castes could never alter their social station. Enlisted men, including my be-medaled grandfather, could never, ever become officers.

My father now enjoyed the adulation of his whole family, with the exception of his mother. She could never come to terms with the trauma of the unwanted life that had unexpectedly taken hold in her young womb, an organ this illiterate heathen would never fully understand. She harboured a lifelong resentment toward him and though I saw them together countless times growing up, I have no memory of either of them speaking a word to each other. Instead she lavished affection on her next child, Ernie, whose arrival two years later was fully legitimate. He would turn out to be a conniving alcoholic wastrel, and neither he nor the next three of her children, albeit more decent people than Ernie, would match my father's prowess by any measure. A few short years later my father, in full army officer dress uniform, walked my mother down the aisle of Walkinstown Parish Church, then out the front doors, to be greeted by an honour guard of fellow army officers, swords raised above their heads to form an arch above the happy couple.

I was conceived that night and nine months later my father led the way in creating a whole new generation of Kennys. When they were married they immediately bought a new semi-detached house in Clondalkin with a proper bathroom, an electric cooker and a tiny wall-mounted fridge in the kitchen and three upstairs bedrooms. We lived there until I was ten and to this day I can draw a map of the village as it was then. We would often go for walks down the Watery Lane, something we were forbidden to do alone, as it followed the course of the Camac to The Grand Canal which was as lethal as ever. Sometimes Dad took us, but usually it was Mom, pushing the latest baby along in front of her. You could fall right into the canal from the towpath, but the fast-flowing Camac had a thicket of blackberry bushes all along its banks. The high walls of the paper mill, where Auntie Nell had worked her whole life, loomed up on the far side.

My friends and I took to fishing for perch in the mill feed ponds behind our school. You were not supposed to but there was a gap in the fence. Here the water was brown, but you could see down a foot or two, whereas after the paper mill had made use of it what flowed alongside the Watery Lane on its way to the sea varied from dishwater grey to an opaque mauve. No new life could swim upriver through such toxic murk and those small perch that we caught must have been descendants of the same fish that would have fed the monks all those centuries earlier.

I was ten when we left Clondalkin, and I was now the oldest of five children just as my father had been. I too was a studious child, by far the best reader in my class. Dad taught Michael and I to play chess. We read so many comics that Mom made us bale them up and take them across the road any time the Rellis sisters were having a jumble sale. Dad subscribed to Time-Life books which provided us with an endless supply of lavishly illustrated hardback volumes about all aspects of nature and science. I learned about the marine iguanas of The Galapagos Islands and studied photos of whaling factory ships. I asked incessantly about evolution only to be told that no-one had ever found the Missing Link that would prove we were descended from apes so we were created by God and we had immortal souls while animals did not.

We moved to Tralee, Count Kerry, for a year, and then back to Dublin, to a custom-built home in Cabinteely, and then to Kill, outside Naas, where I finally grew up, the oldest son of an oldest son, who had done all he could to gain his father's approval, and therefore would brook no other course of action from me. No, I could not go to university and study English just to become a teacher or a journalist. Medicine took far too long, although too long for what went unsaid. Yes, of course I could become a pilot, after I first became an engineer. My mother was no help, as she and Ena mused surreptitiously as to whether I was smart enough to be a Jesuit and not just a Maynooth bog priest. I scored enough points in my Leaving Cert to get into any course in any university in Ireland, but the die was now cast, follow in Dad's footsteps as he had done with his father, or take a leap into the unknown. I had just turned seventeen, life was good, and I would be sailing competitively all that summer.

At the time I believed with all my heart that he had been sincere in his career advice to me. After all, the same path had worked for him. That August Mom and I towed our caravan to the tiny village of Dromineer, Tipperary, on the east shore of Lough Derg with Granny and the other four kids and I spent two glorious weeks racing my little sailing boat against a hundred other identical boats sailed by Irish teenagers who had grown up in a time when sailing clubs had become as ubiquitous as golf clubs. My father never showed up, even for the awards ceremony. We knew he was staying in a rented apartment not very far away in order to be near his latest consulting gig but what we didn't know was that this was also where, like his father before him, he would dally with his wife's sister.

Did he ever mean anything he said? Or was everyone around him just a means to an end? Right up to his own end he held forth to anyone that would listen that there was nothing wrong with polygamy. He never recanted a single word of any of the invective he hurled at all of us. But was this nature or nurture? Was he born with a malicious streak or did he learn it growing up? Tony told a story that one day their father sat his four young sons on top of the monastery wall, stood back and reached out his arms and said: "don't be afraid to jump. I'll catch you." Clearly he could only catch one of the four, but he let them all fall to the ground to skin their knees and howl and then said: "let that be a lesson you. Never trust anyone." And that same war hero was known on occasions to get off the Dublin bus two stops early so as to dally at his wife's sister Auntie Nell's cottage where she lived alone.

My mother was truly saint-like. She loved all five of her children as equally as she could She loved her parents and her dying fathers last words to both her and Ena were that neither of them had ever given him a spot of bother. She loved Ena. She loved everyone and everyone loved her. Dad's mother was nothing like that. Her endlessly repeated advice to me when she had me captive in her kitchen, with gooseberries or rose-hips simmering on the range, was to keep my enemies behind me and my friends in front of me because you always knew who your enemies were but you never knew who your friends were. She was always saying that Ena should go off and find her own man, clearly implying that his evil sister-in-law was to blame for ensnaring her innocent son.

I grew up the oldest son of the oldest son of a revolutionary war hero, though in reality my grandfather had been little more than a child soldier. Aged sixteen when the shooting started, he had saved up for a Mauser rifle, one of those smuggled into Howth Harbour in nineteen-fourteen, when he would have been all of fourteen. He would later be used as an assassin and would be left with life-long PTSD. As a child I often saw him crying while he watched television, projecting his inner torment onto whatever melodrama he hoped would keep his mind off it all. I came of age in post-colonial Ireland with all its contradictions and madness. My family and the whole of Irish society were in turmoil but I was as oblivious to it all as a goldfish is to the fact that it is wet.

At some point when he was still at school my father took carpentry classes, either at the monastery or the library, I am not sure. He made a bookcase that later followed us from home to home. It was about three feet wide by three feet high. It had two vee-shaped shelves plus a flat top. It was stained a very dark colour, like a creosote covered telephone pole. You could still make out the wood grain but not the fact that this was made of pine planks. We filled it up with dozens of little paperbacks, every single Biggles book, and countless Enid Blyton boarding school mysteries, all tilted back at forty-five degrees. I seized possession of this family heirloom at some point and it followed me from Casteknock to Kinsale to Redlands and eventually to a house Peg and I rented in San Jose in the early years of this century.

Haunted by my demoniacal father I became fixated on the bookcase. Mom had not yet died and I had set her up with the best circumstances possible. She had now lived on three years beyond the projections of her doctors on both sides of the Atlantic. But the monster I held responsible for her illness was ever-present, poisoning her, and there was nothing more I could do. She had chosen him over me, over all of us. I stared every day at the dark wooden object that embodied my father's spirit. It was well-made, still rock solid after more than half a century. It might well outlive me, and Justin, and even my future grandson, Kian. But this was no ordinary family heirloom. It had been created by the boy who would become my father. And yet he had never again turned his hands to carpentry, wary perhaps of such proximity to the Nazarene.

It was almost Halloween that year in San Jose, and though the leaves had now all fallen there had been no rain since April. Peg had made fast friends with another mother a few streets away who had two daughters the same ages as Kelly and Charlie, now eight and ten. We went back and forth to each other's homes all the time and on this Friday evening they had invited us over for a bonfire. I was sitting on the bed pulling on my shoes and brooding over my last phone call to Ireland. My mother had assured me, as usual, that everything was fine and that Dad was doing a wonderful job looking after her. But I knew he was ever-present, listening to every word, and that she was speaking as much to him as to me. The more she said such things the more he was compelled to make it so. Which might very well mean it wasn't so at all.

I walked out onto the landing and stared at the bookcase. All the years of not confronting him, of allowing it to come to this, welled up in me. I scooped up the Doctor Seuss books and Disney VCR tapes that now filled the shelves and stacked them against the wall. I wrapped an arm around the top shelf and picked it up. It was as sturdy as ever. I man-handled it into the back of Peg's Jeep and the four of us made the short drive over to Karen's house. The four kids plopped themselves down in the living room to watch Monsters Inc for the umpteenth time. I carried the bookcase around the back where Jim was emptying a barrow full of dry leaves onto the flames that were now beginning to singe the chopped up bough of a lemon tree.

With the children occupied indoors the women lit up cigarettes and Jim passed me a ceramic pipe and a small industrial flamethrower. He grew his own weed in a greenhouse around the side of the house but this was still subject to omertà, even though as far as I could tell, most people, including my own kids and all of their friends, were regular pot smokers. The logs steamed, then the bark peeled away and burned, and finally the wood ignited. Jim and I tossed more logs and leaves on until the flames were about waist high. The women and I drank white wine and Jim passed around shots of tequila.

Finally, when we judged the flames were at their peak, I picked up the bookcase and flung it on. The weight crushed the rest of the wood and sent up an enormous shower of red sparks. Most of these houses went back to a time when the most popular type of roof was wood shakes and had there been a wind we might well have torched the neighbourhood. The fire subsided for a while but then the creosote began to blister. Small tongues of blue flame came to life and ran along the edges of the wood until the entire outline was burning. The logs and the planks exchanged their heat and the crackling grew louder.

The bookcase slowly turned grey. As the centre turned to ash Jim poked the sides into the middle of the fire. Flames danced into the air from all parts of what was left as if the fire itself were celebrating its own destructive power. But there was no banshee howl of pain, no murmurs from the surrounding darkness, and the fire settled down until there were just glowing embers to look at. How did it make me feel? The obvious question though I have no obvious answer.

Chapter One. 1978

All happy families are alike; each unhappy family is unhappy in its own way.
Anna Karenina
Leo Tolstoy

I would have liked to start this story much closer to the present, but the summer of nineteen seventy-eight is when it all began. I was twenty-two years old, working in Algeria on a pipeline project and had been away from home for the longest time in my life. I had not been with my family for Christmas, which had weighed heavily on me, and now I would finally be reunited with them all after an absence of almost a year. We communicated entirely by letter in those days and so this trip had been planned for many weeks. It was a short hop across the Med from Oran to Alicante, where Dad met me at the airport and we drove to the Costa Brava where they were all staying. I was the oldest of five children. After me came Michael, a little over two years younger, then Mary, two years younger than him, then the much younger Finbarr, now fourteen, still with his head of curls, still the quietest and gentlest of us all, and then Anne, ten years younger than me and as feisty as ever.

Mom and her sister, my Aunt Ena, were there. They were inseparable having grown up with no other siblings. There were photos and old home movies of Dad and the two of them on holidays in the west of Ireland long before I was born, sailing to the Aran Islands on an old Galway Hooker, and of them all doing the hula-hoop some Christmas back in the fifties. There had been many Spanish holidays before this one, picked from the Budget Travel brochure, where the only Spaniards were the waiters and barmen. It was now close to a decade since I had been to Generalissimo Franco's Spain. My teenage years had been spent camping and sailing and going to America and France. I cannot say with certainty the exact location of this beach where Dad and I met up with them, though I see it clearly in my mind's eye, but it must have been either Denia or Benidorm since I would have flown into Malaga had they booked Fuengirola again, or even gone back to Torremolinos, both on The Costa Del Sol. Every Spanish beach is a blinding arc of white sand bordering the azure Mediterranean.

I was expecting that same family that swam and horse-played in the ocean and the resort pool while Dad held court with the two women, my mother and her sister, over pitchers of Sangria, or alcoholic Spanish stew as he called it. When we tired we would read paperback novels, half upright on the deck chairs, having paid our pesetas for the towels, our pink Irish flesh turning lobster red despite all the sunscreen, and then go touring in the rental car the next day while the pain subsided.

Family holidays had their dark side too. Dad, as Mom explained every time, just needed time to unwind, because he worked so hard, because he loved us all so much. He was entitled to a tantrum and a day or two of sulking, and then he was back to dear old Dad, the life of the party, fawned over by his wife and her sister, Ena, who was also his business partner. Everything he said they found hilarious and he effortlessly baited them with outrageous proclamations such as that he could knock on any woman's door and she would want to make dinner for him. The women tut-tutted and told me he didn't mean any of it and then he would be off on some monologue about the British or the Jews or the Church. At home he would shake his head and roll his eyes when we put on Eric Clap-trap and ridicule our blue jeans, our uniform of non-conformity.

That day, my feet burning on the white sand as I listened to the waves lapping rhythmically back and forth, was a turning point in my life. Ena, my cherished aunt, a fixture in my life since my earliest memories, and my mother's sole sibling, was being pushed around in a wheelchair by Mom. She had had cancer for a couple of years at least. I had seen her left arm swell up, bloated, and knew she was being treated for "bone cancer", though it was surely lung cancer from her lifelong habit of smoking two packs of Rothmans a day that had metastasised. Neither she nor her sister nor Dad would admit that she had wilfully, if not foolishly, brought this demise on herself, although in later years they would use it as a salutary warning to all of us about the perils of smoking. Mom cried on and off. Ena was listless, probably on very strong pain medicine.

And then there were Michael and Mary. In their teenage years, coming up behind me, they were often just referred to collectively as Michael and Mary. Ena held them in very low regard. She saw them as the bane of my mother's existence. This was not without some justification. Michael, who was now twenty, had achieved a perfect score in first year math in UCD, failed every other subject, and decided he wanted to do medicine. The only way that could now happen would be to get him into Royal College of Surgeons, a private outfit catering mostly to foreign students from rich families in third-world countries. Mom accomplished that, but now here was Michael on crutches. A few months earlier, while Mom and Dad were both out of the country, he had stolen Mom's Triumph Stag and driven it to a party in Waterford, some hundred miles away, at night, while hammered. At some point he came to a hump back stone bridge, the kind they built across canals and narrow rivers in the age of horse travel, a stone arch that led you steeply up and over the waterway and towpath. Usually, these bridges connect two sections of road that follow the course of the canal itself, such that you have to swerve hard onto them and again in the other direction on the other side. This apparently worked for Michael on the uphill approach, but he was just going too fast to make the next turn, and sailed into the air off the summit of the bridge and down into the front room of a cottage on the far side, breaking one of his legs and, demolishing the front of the house, and reducing Mom's bright red convertible mid-life crisis toy to a mangled lump of steel and rubber.

If Ena and Michael were visibly wounded, Mary was of even more concern to Mom and Dad. I cannot recall how much of all this I knew in advance, but Mary was on major antidepressants having thrown herself in the local canal in an attempted suicide. She was now eighteen but even though we had grown up in the same house I didn't know her well. The four year age gap had been a lot when we were very young and by the time she reached adolescence I was already off to college running with my own clique. She certainly was depressed. She just moped around and slept in her room most of the time. As for the younger two, I did not know how much of all of this they were following. At some point, and I cannot recall if it was that day or later, Mom told me that she had wanted to get psychiatric help for Mary but Dad had flatly refused because it would be on her permanent record and could be used against her later. I wasn't sure what to make of that, it was certainly consistent with Dad's lifelong paranoia about all forms of authority, but many years later I would see all of this in a very different light. The first day ended with Dad taking me aside and pleading with me to come home and help my family and saying Mom could not stand me not being there. It was very unlike him to speak so candidly - about anything - and, whether he was sincere in this supplication to the son he had bullied remorselessly all my life, in the face of this horrendous nexus of tragedy, all of it bearing down on my mother's completely undeserving shoulders there was just no other conceivable course of action.

I came back to Dublin and told my employer I was done with being paid one third of what American engineers earned for doing the very same job. This was not exactly what Dad had in mind, but in truth, after the heady early days in Schenectady, I found the job lonely, had seen enough deserts and jungles, and was glad to be back. Ena died a few weeks later, aged fifty-three. We buried her in the same grave as her mother, Granny Skally, who had died two years earlier. Granny had left everything to Ena and nothing to Mom. Ena now supposedly left everything of hers to Mom, but I knew she had left me her shares in a small manufacturing business she and Dad had helped establish and possibly some money too. She owned a house in Naas that she had bought outright with the proceeds of Granny's house in Walkinstown. She also left behind a very nice little two-door orange Datsun, which I simply purloined. There was very little subsequent talk about her which at the time I put down to the shock of her passing, though later events would put the lie to that. We never visited her grave and to this day I have no idea if anyone ever chiseled her name below that of her mother.

Ena had been a constant in my life, a friend and mentor, who took my side and lifted me up in every sense, never asking anything in return other than the occasional errand, refilling the ice-bucket for her vodka or dad's whiskey, or dashing to the shops for a couple of packs of Rothmans. Michael and I were often dropped off at her house in Walkinstown, where she lived with Granny until Granny died. It was one of an endless sea of tiny two-story homes in back-to-back rows that had been built as some inner city slum clearance project long before I was born. The front had a patch of grass and daisies bounded by iron railings, a single cherry blossom tree grew at its centre and three rose bushes were lovingly tended in a small bed under the window. The back garden was less well kept with grass long enough to allow dandelions to flower and pink rhubarb stalks under the privet hedges that we were forever tasked with trimming. Michael as a child had acute separation anxiety and never bonded with Ena, but I did and she doted on me, taking me to age-inappropriate films, like Carry On Doctor and Carry On Nurse, which caused her to double up with laughter while the double entendre went over my head and all I could remember was the lady with the daffodil stuck up her arse. She always took me Christmas shopping to see the train layout in the basement of Brown Thomas and I always knew on some level that she was behind the wooden boxed set of Lego whose lid became a cityscape, our favourite toy of all time.

There were books in that house, from Teilhard de Chardin to Edna O'Brien, and it was there that I discovered the short stories of Frank O'Connor and she would later buy me those of Sean O'Fáolaoin and Brendan Behan and later the novels of Alistair Maclean, anything to wean me off Superman and Batman comics. She drove me places, and when Dan Nolan came to visit from Connecticut she drove us all over Ireland. She dropped us off at a hostel in Kerry and left us to hike up Ireland's tallest mountain, Carrauntuohill and down the other side, picking us up two days later. I was fifteen and Dan was fourteen. He had a smuggled carton of Marlboro's and I had a fiver from Ena that bought a few rounds of Smithwicks in a mountain shebeen. I should have mourned her more than I did, but a benevolent spinster aunt was of far more value to a boy whose father was obsessed with his work and whose mother was pre-occupied with the four younger siblings and only wanted for me to be an example to the rest of them than the same aunt would have been to this grown man. There had always been that nagging suggestion that I might have a vocation and wouldn't I make a fine Jesuit. And now here I was, easily fulfilling that exemplary role, a college graduate, an engineer, a sailing champion, an increasingly erudite conversationalist, a man of the Irish world. Ena had played no small part in my becoming all of this and she will always remain a part of my every childhood memory a reassuring voice many a night years, even decades, after her own passing.

Dad, now bereft of the woman who really was the business brains to his technical knowhow, began to make more and more erratic decisions. Mom joined the consulting business to backfill for Ena but she had neither the acumen nor the temperament to stand up to Dad. I recall going to Paris to a sort of random conference of management consultants which had the objective of co-operative marketing. And then along came Ronson. A bunch of asset strippers acquired the rights to Ronson's lighters and shavers, but their primary interest was the brand name. This resulted in me flying on the Concorde to New York with Dad and then down to Mexico City where there was some kind of factory, and then for a brief period becoming manager of the Ronson lighter factory on the Isle of Wight during the Falklands War where I earned the nickname Malvinas for my views on British colonialism. I was probably more fortunate to return unscathed than I then realised. At this point I had become the salesperson for the electronics business, acquired a better company car, and spent my days picking up drawings and samples, and eventually purchase orders in the lobbies of the many US multinationals who had set up in Ireland to dodge tax and access the European market.

I was back living at home again which I could tell pleased my mother immensely. Michael came and went but was not there much. Mary had moved out to live in a flat in Dublin with some of her friends. Finbarr and Anne were both at boarding school. The absence of my siblings only magnified my own presence. I was now in every sense my mother's nearest living relative. We lived in a sprawling bungalow on the edge of the tiny village of Kill in County Kildare. From beyond our front hedge we could always hear the muffled roar of passing traffic on one of Ireland's busiest roads. Those using it who lived in Dublin, whose urban sprawl at that time petered out about a dozen miles to the North-East, knew it as the Naas Road. Those who lived in Naas, the county seat of Kildare, and parts beyond, knew it, of course, as the Dublin Road.

We had moved here from Dublin when I was fifteen and Michael and I rode the bus the four miles into Naas every day to school. For me this move had proven to be a great opportunity to re-invent myself from a pimply pubescent nobody to the coolest kid in the class, army surplus jacket, Levis, and hair that flowed in rat-tails over the collars of my paisley shirts. I had a better collection of rock albums than any of these bogmen and soon learned to comport myself as a prophet of fashion, a messenger from the wider world, and to my astonishment soon became that most elusive of all things: popular! I had an ever widening circle of friends, at first just boys from my class at school, but then more of their big families, including their sisters, who had yet more friends, and my social life took flight.

Chapter Two. 1979

 Oh, the Smithwick and the Harpic,
the bottle, draught and keg...
I could never figure out,
how does yer man stay up on the surfboard
after fourteen pints of stout.

Christy Moore

One afternoon, with nothing else to do, I drove into Naas and parked in the triangular area on Main Street made possible by the fact that the facades on both sides of the hump in the road did not line up. If you were driving into town from the Dublin side the street rose up toward the town hall between orderly shop fronts facing each other, but if you were coming toward Dublin from the opposite end of town the shopfronts on your left obeyed this same logic while those on your right drifted further away. Naas, an anglicisation of Nás na Rí, which means the gathering place of kings, had reached the height of its prominence some thousand years earlier and this present day anomaly might well be an unintended consequence of a royal decree from that earlier millennium.

I walked across the road toward Hanrahan's, the coffee shop at the bus stop where we had waited after school in all weather, maybe a couple of hundred times. The boys had no school uniforms but the girls flocked in and out in their burgundy pleated skirts and vee-neck jumpers, all of us joyously oblivious of where life might take us in the next few years let alone in the long years to come after that. Turning right I walked past the town hall, an ugly plastered provincial irrelevance. This building hid Moate Hall, a small theatre and the scene of my first slow dance to the tune of Bye-Bye Miss American Pie. Behind that rose the mound known as the Moate, where the kings of old had actually met. The hill I was now cresting was a shoulder of that summit. I walked past Marum's, a pub with an upstairs lounge whose sole purpose was to cater to underage drinkers, and a few doors further down came to my destination.

Naas boasted a dozen pubs, each with its own unique personality, clientele, bartop, paintwork, lighting, acoustics, odours and urinals. But the crown jewel was Fletcher's public house. I pushed open the huge oak door with its panes of beveled glass and walked into a spotlessly clean room with a tiled floor and a vaulted ceiling. On the walls were mounted some big old metal tea bins, legacy of an earlier time when this had also been a grocery shop. Tommy Fletcher himself was there to greet me with his signature sideways nod as I sidled onto the barstool nearest to the wall. I ordered a pint of Guinness and a pack of five Hamlet cigars. Fletcher's had won Ireland's pub of the year contest more than once. It was airy and bright and the pints were always perfect, a true temple to the art of drinking. What better place to contemplate the recent twists and turns of my life.

It was still less than two years since I had graduated, flying off to Schenectady, New York, to a months long training course as a Field Engineer, with several other classmates. We had been hired by a subsidiary of General Electric which was at that time the worlds largest technology company and this rust-belt town where the Erie Ship Canal met the Hudson River remained a major manufacturing hub a century after Thomas Edison spotted that land for sale sign from his train window. The company set us up with an apartment in an old brownstone in a seedy part of town plus a couple of rental cars to get to and from the factory and the training campus. To us this was paradise.

The bars were like nothing back home. You didn't sit around muttering politics and buying rounds of pints. The beer, Schlitz, Pabst or Genesee, came in pitchers, and you shared it with girls who played pool or shuffleboard or coin-operated basketball hoops with us. Women's lib had prevailed, AIDS had yet to be discovered, love was free and condoms were optional. One Saturday night I hooked up with a buxom nurse who brought me back to her apartment, yet another dingy brownstone, where she assured me the previous tenant, and not her, had installed the ceiling mirror tiles over the bed. She wasn't just uninhibited, I doubt she could spell, or even define the word. Candles and mirrors and incense and a few last tokes with a roach clip and we watched ourselves on our own silver screen until when we were done she turned to me and said: "Thank you, that was great." Indeed it obviously had been, not just to me, but to her neighbours above and below who could not have failed to hear. But in my wildest imaginings I could never have conjured up an Irish girl actually verbalising her gratitude for helping her achieve a couple of orgasms. Wouldn't I be the lucky fellow that she had allowed between the sheets with her in the first place?

But this wonderland of breakfasts in American diners, wet tee-shirt contests, one-night stands and rock concerts was not contributing to the bottom line of Generous Electric and one by one we were sent off on actual assignments. I was sent to Venezuela to work on one of a program of rural electrification projects. I was billeted in a hotel in Maracaibo with the rest of the team and every day we commuted around the lake to the town of Ciudad Ojeida where we were technical advisors to the construction company installing four GE gas turbines. Barefoot children wandered about selling mangos and fruit juice while the guard dog slept in the shade under the site trailer. I set up my dial indicators on the steel feet that had themselves been precisely set into the surface of a newly poured foundation.

Since GE operated its own travel agency anyone they sent to this town for any reason ended up in the same hotel by default. There were Americans, Brits, and me. There was even a female American engineer and those were about as common as unicorns in those days. Linda was probably in her mid-twenties, though she could have passed for sixteen with her long silky blonde hair and waifish frame. She glommed onto the group, more for protection than companionship it seemed, but she took to talking to me while she read and tanned herself by the pool. She watched me dive and told me to keep my ankles together and then as our banter progressed I learned that she had been raised in the Bahia faith, a religion I had never heard of.

The pool shut at dusk every night as the jungle erupted into a cacophony of chirps and screeches and you had to swat away flying beetles and whatever else came alive in the dark. indoors there was another lounge, but no entertainment and the televisions in the rooms played a handful of Spanish language stations. But Linda had her own ideas for passing the hours between sunset and slumber. She was oblivious to the Bahai prohibition on premarital sex. And she had clearly been absent on the day the class was taught the lesson about pursuing a chaste and holy life. If she had ever heard the teachings of moderation in sexual matters she had long since discarded them. For Linda, sex was a gymnastic performance, a sequence of positions and moves that varied from night to night but always with same goal in mind. Some nights she climaxed easily, leaving plenty of time for a second and third act, but other nights try as she might, and regardless of every permutation of foreplay, she would end up having to take the matter into her own hand.

All of this nocturnal activity was very furtive, for two reasons. First, the hotel owners, a couple of German men, probably not old enough to actually be Nazis in exile, were nevertheless very vigilant against their premises being used like this, and second neither of us wanted the rest of the all male entourage to know anything. She was a woman making her way in a man's world and I certainly was not going to rock the boat on her. For Linda this was entirely transactional. Indeed, one night after a long hot day, and too much Venezuelan beer, I was just not up for whatever gymnastics she had in mind. I dozed off while she was sitting on top of me. I could feel her getting more and more agitated and then suddenly her tiny hand delivered a stinging slap to my face. Though I was now fully awake I feigned nodding off again and watched through eye slits as Linda leapt from the bed, pulled her tight denims up over her tiny ass, then bent over so as to pull her top over her hair and torso in one move, shook her mane down her back, grabbed her undies and stormed off.

She returned the next night and we resumed where we had left off as if nothing had happened. Her trip was coming to an end and one bad night was hardly enough to take the risk of changing horses, at least such were the calculations of this golden-haired sexaholic. Then one morning she was gone and I never saw or heard from her again. By now the rest of the crew were making serious inroads into Maracaibo night-life and it was not long before we were all piling into the rental cars on the weekends to take a bevy of muchachas to the beach at the mouth of the lake. A carefree Latina girl fed me the eyes of the fish we bought from a grill shack, the wind held the sandflies at bay, and the occasional foot long dragonfly hovered slowly by.

Tommy Fletcher proffered my second perfectly poured pint with his usual mixture of obsequiousness and pride of ownership as I lit my third cigar. After Maracaibo I was sent to Libya to rendezvous with an Irish maintenance crew. The terminal stank at Tripoli airport. Armed soldiers watched over the baggage claim area, all the signs were in Arabic only, and without our handler with his cardboard sign we would have been totally lost. We loaded into some cars and sped toward the city centre, first along a well paved road and then zigzagged through roadworks, past half-finished buildings and were eventually disgorged in front of an apartment building that we were told belonged to the oil company, which meant it belonged to Gaddafi and his cronies.

We spent three miserable days, giving blood so they could test us for venereal disease, eating really bad food in dingy dining rooms, served up by a sullen staff, none of whom could have had a bath for at least a month, and then finally were driven back to the airport to board an old Fokker Friendship. We sweltered in the heat as it droned out over the sand dunes and were deafened by the noise of the turboprop engines, eventually coming to land at an oilfield somewhere in the Sahara Desert. I was assigned to a trailer that I shared with one of the Irish mechanics. We worked seven days a week, great for those paid by the hour, and ate three meals a day in the cafeteria. After dinner we all retired to what was called The Clubhouse, three trailers pushed together to form what was effectively a Western embassy. No Libyans were allowed across the threshold and I was told that all of the oilfields had one of these. Here there were pool tables, dartboards and a bar. There was a still hidden out of sight in the corner that produced grain alcohol, which the workers called Flash. Your choice of alcoholic beverages was Flash and Coke or Flash and Fanta. Sleep, eat, work, eat, work, eat, drink Flash and repeat.

After that I returned to Schenectady, in the dead of winter, where my Robert Redford moustache routinely froze as I walked across the parking lot from the offices to the turbine factory. None of my old mates were there to hang out with now and I was glad when I was assigned to a pipeline project in Algeria. I was the third start-up engineer to attempt to bring the four turbines at Station Three, a few miles outside the town of Laghouat, into operation. We stayed in a house near the centre of town and on hot nights we pulled our beds up onto the roof. Rumour had it that the previous occupants, Russian army officers, had all had their throats cut one night for messing with the local girls. I walked around the old part of town many evenings after work but I saw no girls, just old men sitting on stone steps playing backgammon. It was an ancient Arab town, and if you continued south away from the Atlas mountains, where we passed Bedouin camps every day on the day to work, you would eventually come to Timbuktu where they said you could still eat human flesh.

All this brings us back to page one and that fateful day on the beach in Spain. If that had not happened there is no question but that I would have just continued bouncing from one assignment to the next like all my buddies. But now, given a choice, what was the better course? I was fortunate to have a family business to look to, but what of now living in Ireland indefinitely? If the future was full of the pleasures of the Americas then Ireland seemed a poor choice. But on my last trip to Schenectady I had wandered up and down the test stands reading the paperwork for every turbine that told you who the customers were and it seems to me from this and from word seeping back from my peers that most of the export orders were coming from The Middle East. Saudi Arabia, Iraq, The Gulf States. You would be mopping your brow and dreaming of Sally O'Brien and a pint of Harp like the fellow in the TV ad.

As Tommy and I exchanged knowing nods and he readied my third pint I made my mind up. I would stay here on the island of saints and scholars and make a go of it. But this conclusion left me with the strange feeling of being out of step with the world. Everyone I knew had moved on but here I was choosing to stay put and to do so indefinitely. Was life now passing me by? As Tommy slid the third pint across the bar I lit the last Hamlet cigar. It dawned on me then that even within the context of Ireland I was out of step. The town of Naas was where I had come of age, making it the only place I could truly call home. And Naas was where the two Irelands met. The Pale ran right through Naas, possibly right underneath Tommy Fletcher's bar, maybe even right beneath the barstool I was sitting on. Yes, it was entirely possible that my right leg was inside The Pale while my left leg was outside The Pale, since I was facing North-East.

Back in the twelfth century, the king of Leinster had brought in a mercenary army of Normans from England to help him with some war and with their chainmail and crossbows they soon conquered the entire country. But over time they intermarried with the Gaelic families and became more Irish than the Irish themselves. To remedy this a succession of English kings sent one army after another to impose English law. Eventually matters came to a stalemate. The English erected an earthen berm stating at a point on the east coast about twenty miles south of Dublin that came inland as far as Naas where it swung north eventually bending back to the east coast about thirty miles north of Dublin. This was called The Pale. As child I always thought this was a palisade of pointed sticks like some enormous cowboy fort, but it wasn't. It was designed as a deterrent to raiding parties, to slow them down in both directions while soldiers were marched out from Dublin.

The Pale stood the test of time and gave rise to the expression Dublin Jackeen, meaning those of us who lived under the hated Union Jack flag and to the equally pejorative term Culchy, meaning someone who lived outside The Pale. This is actually a bastardisation of an Irish word, Chualtaigh, meaning people who live in the countryside. To this day it is easy to distinguish a Jackeen with his Dublin accent from a Culchy raised in Counties Wicklow, Kildare, or WestMeath, no more than twenty miles apart. But I was now half Dublin and half Kildare, neither fish nor foul. To my old Dublin friends there was now a provincial air about me, whereas to my new Naas friends I would always be a blow-in. There it was, I was out of step even before all this started.

"One for the road, Tommy!", I called down the long bar.

Chapter Three. 1979 - 1983.

 *Oh, sweet are the dreams as the dudeen I puff,*

Of whisperings over the sea,
Come back, Paddy Reilly to Ballyjamesduff,
Come back Paddy Reilly to me.

Percy French

Enter, or rather re-enter, Kate. We had met when she was in Fifth Year and I was in Sixth Year in Naas, ages fifteen and sixteen. We were both blow-ins, me a Jackeen whose Dad bought a big house in the country in Kildare, she the oldest daughter of a senior Garda (police officer), who had relocated from Limerick on the heels of a promotion. We were both oldest children of big families with ambitious fathers and so it fell on both of us to be the responsible ones. We accomplished this while leaving time for other pursuits, such as hitch-hiking to Achill Island and having non-stop sex in cheap bed and breakfasts for a week looking out at the wind and rain. Soon after I started at UCD Kate moved to London to live with a bevy of other Irish girls all pursuing their dreams of becoming a nurse, that ticket to independence in what were still very patriarchal times. We drifted apart. I met up with her one summer on the way back from picking grapes in Bordeaux and we took a bus to Brighton for more wonderful sex in a cheap hotel. Whatever the connection was between us, so far, it stood the test of time and distance.

Now I was back in Ireland and for all my gallivanting, no less in love with her. She had had her own summer adventures in campsites from France to Egypt and back again. We might be a pair of old flames by now but the magic was still there, though Kate had not returned specifically because of me. The Irish girls she had lived with in London while she trained as a nurse were one by one fleeing the nest, returning to various parts of Ireland where there were plenty of jobs now that they had been trained in Britain. When I heard she was back in Naas we hooked up again and took a trip to Tenerife for what was an incredibly romantic getaway. We stayed in a half-board hotel that we had picked out of the travel agency brochure where the buffet included something called pulpo, pickled octopus salad. We lay on volcanic black sand beaches and frolicked in the warm surf. We rented a dune buggy and toured the whole island, marvelling at the banana plantations, then freezing in our beachwear on the ascent to the volcano. We were a couple again as much in love as ever, but in a deeper more meaningful way, two successful young people with an eye to the future. Kate, now a qualified nurse, moved back to Ireland, got a job in Saint James's Hospital in Dublin and set herself up in a flat nearby.

Life evolved into pub culture with other couples and parties and regattas with the Blessington Sailing Club crowd after I rejoined and bought a Laser, a hugely popular cat-rigged one-man racing dinghy back then. Life was truly great and one night I took Kate to The Mirabeau Restaurant in Sandycove, a place so pretentious it had neither prices nor menus, then proposed to her walking along the pier by Bullock Harbour afterwards. That didn't go too well as she hadn't seen it coming, but we soon became engaged anyway, and had a perfect traditional wedding in September 1980. The groom's party wore top hats and Aston grey tails, and the bride arrived at the church in a silver Rolls royce. There was a banquet and speeches in the Keadeen Hotel, a few miles outside Naas. We had a brief haphazard honeymoon in Portugal, with balmy nights of love-making in a different seaside hotel every night. Then in early 1981 we flew to the US for a real honeymoon, meeting friends in Boston and Connecticut before flying to Florida to experience the newly opened Disneyworld.

By this time Michael had abandoned the field of medicine, done a stint selling encyclopedias, and was now involved in Dad's latest enterprise, selling what would soon be known as personal computers. Mary had a steady boyfriend, John Harney, younger brother of my very first girlfriend. They ran in their own circle of friends and we saw very little of them other than at mandatory family get-togethers where Dad continued to hold court but with far less panache in the absence of one of his two biggest fans. Since Ena took no part whatsoever in the cooking and catering she had provided a full time audience for Dad's incessant postulating, his rhetorical questions, his dire predictions about the British monarchy, his vitriol against those bloody farmers ruining the country, the occasional tirade against those artsy-fartsy queers running Telefís Eireann, and a reminder that Gay Byrne couldn't speak a lick of Irish and had even failed his Leaving Cert.

Mary would sometimes provide him with a foil by asking why we always just talked about business and politics and not about people but the patriarch was still more than capable of bending that around by merely overemphazising her name as though she were not present and we needed to be reminded whose laughable idea we had just heard while Mary sat there, pulling on her cigarette, condemned to irrelevance. Mary was now twenty years old but in her father's mind she was still just an amusing, if not very clever, child. Finbarr was now sixteen and Anne fourteen, so they had memories of Ena, but they were too young to remember the glory days when we transitioned from being an ordinary Irish family living in a semi-detached house in Clondalkin, the village Dad grew up in that was now essentially a Dublin suburb, to this, a sprawling country bungalow, with the nearest neighbour separated by an acre of lawn.

Ena had been key to that transformation. The older of the two daughters, she was sent to teacher training college and rose to be Principal of a primary school in a working class Dublin neighbourhood, no small feat for a woman not of the cloth in those days. Granny Skally, her mother, was horrified when she chucked this in to go into business with Dad. But it all worked out. Dad had been working in the field of industrial engineering, first for a British company, then for an American one, and had figured out that this so-called Management Consulting really had no entry barriers nor did it require any capital to get going, just a business card with lots of letters after your name. Ena ran the office, Dad did the consulting, and the fees flowed in. They hired more consultants, then moved to the house in Kildare and built a suite of offices onto it. They were really efficiency experts, licensing a technique from Dad's previous employer, with whom they maintained close connections, and there was now a steady flow of American visitors to our house.

Those were exciting times. Dad and Ena held court in the living room while it was my job to ensure a steady flow of ice cubes for the Americans for their drinks. It was here that the exchange scheme between us and the Nolan kids was concocted, resulting in Dan Nolan's Kerry hosteling and a subsequent six weeks for me in Connecticut. Bob Nolan soon went out on his own too and was even more successful. I visited them a few times while I was working in Schenectady and the whole crew of them passed through one Christmas on a skiing trip to Switzerland. Kate and I had agreed on a second honeymoon to make up for the Portugal debacle and we started that off at the Nolan home. I was planning to head to Niagara Falls next, but the Nolans talked us out of that, saying we should fly to Florida to a new theme park in Orlando called Disney World, which we did and which everyone assured us was even better than the original in California, a part of the world still far beyond our horizon.

Mary's flirtation with a self-inflicted watery death was now all but forgotten. Somewhere along the way she had dropped out of school and when she tried to resume again the nuns were having none of it. How could they be sure she had not left to have a baby out of wedlock, rich immoral Dublin blow-in that she was? The Sisters of Mercy would have no truck with any such scandal, whether or not there was any truth to the rumours. Mary rounded out her secondary school at a private college in Dublin and found a clerical job. She rented a flat with a few of her friends and passed into adulthood. She turned twenty-one, going steady with John, when all of a sudden they announced that they were getting married. Mom booked The Hibernian Hotel on Dawson Street, where she and Dad had their own reception long, long ago. It was a great event, though Kate was put out that John's sister Rose was seated at the same table as us. It didn't bother me, it was the first time I tasted Baked Alaska. And then, a few months later, Rex Harney was born. My sister had morphed from a troubled teenager, almost taking her own life, to young wife and mother in the short space of three years. Mom's oft repeated desire to see her children settle down around her and produce grandchildren was beginning to take shape.

Soon after Kate's return to Ireland we mulled over my moving in with her but when I broached the subject with my parents there was such an explosive reaction from my father that I backed off. It was a classic example of the power dynamics of our family. When I told Mom what I was thinking she quietly demurred and waited for an opportunity to raise the subject with only the three of us in the room. This I now saw was the price of working in a family business "What kind of example would that set for the rest of the family?" he roared, leaving no room to manoeuvre. Partly on foot of this we brought forward our own wedding plans and then moved into Ena's house in Naas which my mother had inherited. This further aggravated our dependency on them even though we paid fair rent. And that led us to buy the house in Castleknock, a burgeoning fashionable suburb of Dublin just west of The Phoenix Park. But this was a stretch for us and the mortgage ate up most of our cash. Still, it was a good stepping stone for us on the way to our eventual goal of building a bungalow on a piece of land in Wicklow with a view of the mountains, like the homes of the doctors and lawyers where Kate had babysat as a teenager. I would cycle out to meet her, spend a few hours heavy petting on the couch, and cycle home later, always with a case of blue balls that really hurt with every pedal.

Less than a year after Rex was born Kate gave birth to our own son, Justin. By this time we were living in Casteknock, painting, decorating and doing up the garden. This was a much easier work commute for both of us though I still spent a lot of my time traveling around the country. Our customers were the multinational electronic manufacturers, for whom we made small sub-assemblies, and who were deliberately scattered around the country in small industrial parks at the edges of towns and villages in the hope of both reducing the double-digit unemployment that grew exponentially worse the further you got from Dublin and curtailing the resulting emigration and depopulation of rural Ireland that had been going on since the Great Famine.

Justin's arrival was not exactly planned, but it was not unwelcome either. Kate reckoned we conceived him on New Year's Eve in 1982, which had indeed been a night of beer-swilling debauchery leading up to the usual mayhem as the crowds rang in the New Year at Christchurch. He was a boisterous child and as soon as he was able would fling himself out over the bars of his cot. We got him his own bed but this in turn meant locking him into his bedroom so he would not fall down the stairs. For the first several nights of this we would listen until we knew he was asleep then I would creep up the stairs, unlock the door and push it open sliding him across the floor with it. After a few weeks he accepted his lot and for the rest of his childhood he went to bed willingly every night without ever having any specific bedtime.

Ireland in the nineteen-eighties was a highly conflicted society. The economy was not growing fast enough to provide jobs for all the children of families of five or more such as our own and emigration continued unchecked. The hunger strikes in Belfast had led to an upsurge in violence in Northern Ireland and when we drove up there to buy cheaper petrol and groceries we were greeted by fortified border crossings and black flags hanging from the telephone poles. Down south we were at the vanguard of a rejection of Catholic doctrine, abandoning the Sunday mass attendance of our childhood. Life was hard for most people but we had it good and we knew it. We ate out and took mini-breaks to newly built holiday cottages in Clare and Galway. We basked in the natural beauty all around us never out of sight of the stone ruins of castles and monasteries and even more ancient dolmens and stone circles all of which were our heritage. We lived in a magical time and place and when we thought about the future there wasn't a cloud in the sky.

Chapter Four. 1983 - 1984

For everything that's lovely is
But a brief, dreamy, kind delight.

William Butler Yeats

I was now Managing Director of our little manufacturing business. Ena's old friend who had run it from the beginning took off to start her own business right after my wedding, a backhanded wedding present as I saw it. There was a ritual in those days that you had to show up in a suit in the customer's lobby and wait patiently for the buyer that you dealt with to come out with the next round of purchase orders. This proved that you were serious about the business and could be relied upon to do quality work and deliver on time. The return trip from Cork, Limerick or Shannon would always take me past Mom and Dad's house and if time allowed I would swing by for a cup of tea and to report how things were going.

There was no practical way to give them advance notice of this or to know who would be there. The Management Consultants spent very little time in the office as that meant they were not earning fees. There was a small staff now managed by Mom, Nessa O'Connor, who was Dad's secretary and Mary Mullen, who did the books. On this particular wintry afternoon in late nineteen-eighty-three there were only two cars there, Dad's big mustard yellow Merc, and Nessa's little hatchback. I tried the front door of the house but it was locked. I walked around to the kitchen door, also locked. They must be working in the office I thought, and walked over to that end of the building, but peering through the vertical blinds in the big plate glass windows I could see no-one and the office door was also locked.

They must all be off at a meeting somewhere else I concluded and walked back to my Peugeot. Just as a I sat into it I saw Dad coming to the outer glass doors of the porch clutching a towel around him. His hair was dripping wet and I noticed for the first time just how old he looked, shoulders rounded, arm muscles slack, no longer the spritely ex-army officer who lectured us about our posture and made us sleep as small children with our arms outside the blankets.

"Sean, I didn't see you there, come on in, I was just taking a shower."

Taking a shower? In the middle of a weekday afternoon? Most Irish people still took baths and daily showers were the stuff of Hollywood.

"I think there might be some beer in the fridge," he went on, "Just let me get some clothes on."

The front lounge of the house was two steps lower than the rest of the floors, still with the thick red carpet of the previous owners, the white couches from the old house in Cabinteely, a beaten brass oval coffee table from Lebanon, red velvet drapes and an inlaid Damascus side table that opened out into either a chess board or a card table. An undersized art print hung from a nail above the fireplace that had been in the wall when they bought the house. The mantelpiece held still more brass ornaments and African carvings.

If those walls could talk. All those Christmases with endless games of Scrabble and Monopoly, followed by Stephen's Day when we would go and bring the grandparents and grandaunts and granduncles and ply them with sherry and the photos before the debs dances. And those times that Dad had reduced me to tears. It hadn't been my fault that Christmas when Ena lit the fire and the room filled up with smoke. I was the one who climbed onto the roof and tried to poke the bird's nest down with a long plank and it just slipped out of my hand. His temper was so out of control that I left and marched down to the village, never wanting to return, but Ena eventually found me and she and Mom told me to be the bigger man and go in and apologise to him and then I had to get back up on the roof and lower string down with a weight, so he could hook it over the plank and I could pull it back up.

I found a bottle of Carlsberg and poured it into a glass. The world had yet to accept drinking by the neck. Coffee mugs were only then replacing cups and saucers. Dad returned fully dressed and poured himself a neat Powers Whiskey. He sat in his armchair but his body language was all wrong. He didn't cRex his legs or sip on his whiskey while he gathered his thoughts.

"I better not stay long," I said, "Kate is expecting me." I wanted to get this lie in up front.

"Actually I was just killing time while Nessa is typing up a report for me."

"Yeah, I saw her car."

"Sure, why don't we go down to the office and say hello."

And with that we walked down the corridor that led past the bedrooms and into the adjoining offices, drinks in hand. Sure enough, Nessa sat at her desk in her typist's chair pounding away at her IBM golfball typewriter. She was wearing a headset since she was typing out what Dad had dictated earlier. Nessa avoided all eye contact, simply acting as if we were not there and we returned to the house.

I mumbled some stuff about work, Dad asked about Kate, and I left, my mind racing. How old was Nessa? Would you call her a spinster? She had a few strands of grey hair, but that more confirmed that she was not yet old enough to need to get her hair dyed every other week. When does your hair start to turn grey anyway? I had no idea. As for Dad's age I didn't keep track of it, but I could figure it out. I was twenty-seven, so he was in his mid-fifties. Did people still have sex when they were that old? I couldn't be sure about that either. They certainly didn't have babies at that age. I drove home in a daze and said nothing to Kate about it. It was just one more of those things you have to try to forget about. Sweep it under the rug. Pull your socks up and move on.

Kate was again pregnant and this time it had been thoroughly planned and discussed. We had agreed to have just two children in keeping with our belief in zero population growth. Since we had a boy we were now hoping for a girl in which case I would get to name her. We were also concerned that if we had another boy he would have second son syndrome, like Michael. Though he and I had spent our early years going to and from school together every day, we grew entirely apart by the time our school days ended. He resented my success and believed I was given much more favourable treatment. I believed the complete opposite. He had me as an example while I had no one. He could beat me at chess and he was better than me at math. No one but me sat all those Leaving Cert exams, got into UCD, endured four years of Calculus and came out the other end with a degree in Engineering. He had every bit, and more, exposure to sailing, since he started earlier. They even bought him his own boat. He could have pursued the same summer jobs, but he didn't. He played pool, he flunked out of everything, crashed the car and broke his legs. None of this was my fault.

We knew with some certainty that we had conceived this new baby one warm September night on a sandy beach on the island of Crete, listening to the waves crashing as the Libyan Sea glistened in the moonlight. And so, that cold night in the Spring of nineteen-eighty-four, a very pregnant Kate eschewed the wine from the magnum on the table in our dining room where we were feeding our two English sailing club friends, Mike and Edith, this new-found Mexican fare, called tacos. They were a few years older than us, with three young girls, and well on their way to making their fortune by dominating the Irish market for indoor house plants. Justin was fast asleep upstairs. We had just served up the meal when the doorbell rang, which was very unusual this late. There stood my mother on the porch, sobbing uncontrollably.

"Mom, what's happened?"

She tried to hold back the sobs but was only able to get her words out in a quivering voice, punctuated every other word with more sobs.

"Your (sob) father (sob) walked out on me. (sob) In a restaurant."

"What? How did you get here?"

"He threw (sob) the car keys at me."

I looked out at the street and sure enough the mustard Merc was parked behind Mike's car.

"Come on in. We're just sitting down to dinner with Mike and Edith Lawrence."

"Oh, I'm so sorry, I didn't know you had visitors."

Neither Kate nor the visitors could hear any of this because I had closed the kitchen door to keep the heat in when I opened the front door.

"It's fine. Sounds like you've eaten."

This was anything but fine. The presence of my hysterical mother would put an end to the amusing banter the four of us had been enjoying so far.

"Sean, I just have to talk to someone."

The crying now returned worse than ever. Whatever row had unfolded it had left my mother clearly devastated. Usually when Dad flared up I became the object of his rage. But I had not been there to bear the brunt of this one.

"Maybe you should just go upstairs and lie down and we'll talk in the morning," I suggested. That would solve everything.

"No, no. I didn't know you had visitors. That wouldn't be fair to Kate."

This was an idiotic argument but this was not a rational person. Besides, any minute now and Kate would be out to investigate.

"Mom, please come in so I can close the door. It's freezing."

"Maybe we could just go for a drive?" She proffered a set of car keys that I had not noticed up till now. I returned to the others, explained to them that it was my mother, she was in a state, and needed to get stuff off her chest. I would take her for a drive in The Phoenix Park and be back in about half an hour. Go ahead and eat and don't wait for me. Just one of those things. I went back out to the hall, took the keys, pulled on my American goose-down jacket and walked with my still bawling mother to Dad's car.

"I'm so sorry, but I just have no one else to talk to," she said as I started the car.

Mom took a few deep breaths and wiped her eyes with a tissue. We had not yet reached the Castleknock Park gate when she said: "I think your father is having an affair with Nessa. And when I confronted him about it he denied everything and just stormed off,"

So that was what this was all about. Should I act surprised? But Dad knew I knew. He probably didn't know Mom had made a beeline to me after he left the restaurant. They didn't go out much together, so this was probably a ruse to get him on neutral ground one on one for exactly the purpose of confronting him in a safe public place.

"What makes you think that?" I asked.

"She just started acting very strangely around me. And why didn't he move her up to the factory with everyone else? All these reports that she had to do in the office and that he had to be there for. And always when I am out shopping or playing golf. I know something is off. And his furious reaction just now reeks of guilt."

We drove through the park gates. Gone now were the houses and streetlights. As Dubliners it is one of our proudest boasts that we have the largest park of any city in Europe. It hosts a herd of deer, our President's residence, a horse racing track, and Dublin Zoo. Most of it is unlit, but what is still noticeable is the absence of the stone walls and iron railings that characterise the city itself. It is mostly a flat grassy plain and there was not a soul around. Should I tell her? Before I could decide she resumed both talking and crying.

"You do know that your father was having an affair with Ena behind my back for God knows how long."

I slowed the car down. Had I heard this right? My mother's sister, my beloved Aunt Ena, had been having sex with my father? This couldn't be right. This made no sense. Ena had been a part of all of our lives for my whole life. She had been a part of Dad's life going back to when they were teenagers. There were black and white photos of the three of them on a Galway Bay Hooker, the last sailing boats that had worked the Aran Islands. They did everything together. But he had married Doreen, not Ena. And both of my parents had told me numerous times that they had both gone to the altar virgins. How could this possibly have happened?

"What? What makes you think that?" I asked, in complete disbelief.

"I caught them at it. In the office one day."

I couldn't breathe. I pulled over and got out. I walked around the car onto the grass. This couldn't be happening. Ena went to Mass every Sunday and had never stopped that I knew of. In the space of a few seconds everything I thought I knew about the world I thought I lived in had been shattered into a million pieces. I started to retch, and then I vomited so violently my throat burned. I shook uncontrollably and clutched my knees to steady myself. Eventually there was nothing else to eject. I inhaled a few deep breaths of the cold night air and walked back to the car.

"I'm sorry, I thought you knew," said my mother as I sat back into the driver's seat.

"No, no, I didn't. But you're right," I told her, "Dad is screwing Nessa. I caught them at it."

Now the wailing came back in force. "I don't understand. What does she have that I don't have? Ena died before we could come to terms with it. She told me she knew she was going to go straight to hell."

It was now going on almost six years since Ena's death. Mom shook her head from side to side and continued crying as we drove back to the house. There were no more revelations, as if there could not possibly be more to say that would rival this, and we lapsed into silence. When we arrived back Mike's car was gone.

"Do you want to stay the night?" I asked.

"No, no. You have enough going on and Kate has her hands full. I'll be fine."

She drove off, ever the martyr, far from fine, and I found Kate in the kitchen cleaning up. I was too exhausted to put any sort of spin on any of this and told her more or less verbatim the night's revelations.

Chapter Five. 1984

Gerry Rafferty

Our family was not wealthy by any modern measure, but we were better off than most. Ireland was in the throes of a years-long recession. Unemployment exceeded seventeen percent and it would have been far worse were it not for a century and a half of relentless emigration which kept the population static. By this time Dad had wound down his consulting practice and was all in on growing our little manufacturing business. There was good reason for this. The economy had been propped up due to the influx of mostly American-owned factories. These businesses were lured by non-existent profits tax, more or less free factories, training grants for everyone they hired, low-interest loans and leases, and access to the European market.

Local business owners reckoned that what was good for the goose was good for the gander, and a similar web of benefits now emerged for anyone starting a manufacturing business. But what to make? We simply took in electronic laundry from the likes of Apple Computer and a host of now extinct makers of printers and monitors and mini-computers. Mostly we made cable assemblies but we also repaired telephones and soldered together simple circuit boards. There were lots of similar companies making all kinds of sub-assemblies for the multinationals, and the government now looked for ways to transform some of us into makers of real products.

Technology transfer became the order of the day, and Dad spent his time finding such opportunities. He went to Japan and came back with the possibility of licensing keyboards for computers. The Ronson shaver and lighter opportunity came and went. We came up with a design for a car telephone, and made a few. Inventors came in and out of our conference room. But what my father was really focused on was gaining access to this slush fund of grants and soft loans. He didn't take any part in the actual activity of finding actual orders. He sat in his office writing a ten-year business plan for how this would multiply the size of our business.

I do not recall where he was the Monday morning after my mother's visit, but she showed up and came into my office and closed the door.

"Your father and I had a long talk when he got home," she began. There was no explanation as to how he got home. "And he assures me there was nothing going on between him and Nessa. You must have just been confused."

I had always known Dad's younger brother, my uncle Tony, was a philandering rogue, and when he hit on our very pretty, and very married, red-haired receptionist I had called him at his flat, where he spent some of the week away from home, only to be answered by some other floozy. I shook my head. Now I knew this ran in the family.

"Then why did it take him a month to attend a couple of meetings in Japan?"

"I don't know," she replied, "but your father is one of the best businessmen around. He was doing all of this long before you."

This was about to be proven to be a highly debatable statement. On one occasion he had taken me out for a pint, a rare event since he mostly drank his own whiskey in his own living room, and confessed, secure in the knowledge of my ignorance, that he had made a lot of bad decisions ever since Ena had died. We were not a family that expressed our feelings well, if at all. But by not doing so my mother was now doing so. After her bout of crying on Friday night she seemed to have concluded that she had had her revenge and this was all now behind her. Dad had sworn to her that nothing had happened, which was what she wanted to hear, even though she knew that what she was really getting was an assurance that it would not happen again.

"Now, your father implored me to come and see you and to tell you not to say anything about any of this to Kate or he would just be mortally ashamed to ever be in the same room with her again."

Kate was certainly held in very high esteem by everyone but this was balderdash.

"She's my wife so I tell her everything." This was not entirely true, but what did my mother think that Kate and I would talk about all weekend?

There was an intake of breath. "Your father is going to be very upset."

And she left. Ena had been the business brains behind the consulting business but this manufacturing business had been the brainchild of a long-standing Legion of Mary friend of hers, Lily Rafferty. This religious organisation had been founded by one Frank Duff and attracted young women like my mother, Ena, her friend Carmel, Lily, and a raft of like minded socially conscious young Catholics. Duff's lay organisation made great strides in assisting inner city prostitutes who were really no more than unfortunate girls who had been abandoned by their families and boyfriends upon becoming pregnant. Perhaps less justifiably Duff's Legion also went to great lengths to replace the Protestant soup kitchens with Catholic ones.

Lily worked for possibly the very first Irish electronic contract manufacturer as a supervisor over their cable harness shop. They were going bankrupt, but several of their customers wanted the work of Lily and her department to just continue without interruption. One night in nineteen-seventy four Lily and the buyer from her biggest and most lucrative customer came to the house with an idea. They would all start a new business. Dad and Ena would put up the money for thirty percent each, Fergus, the buyer, would send all the orders their way in exchange for a twenty percent stake, and Lily, also with a twenty percent share, would take all of her staff with her and run this new company. And now here we were ten years later.

By this point, Fergus had forfeited his shares by taking out a loan from the company and Lily was likewise toast since she was now a competitor. Ena had long promised to leave me her shares in her will, which would have made Dad and I equal partners but that was never going to happen and in the end Dad and Mom magnanimously gave me a twenty percent stake without any reference to Ena whatsoever.

A few weeks after the Ena and Nessa denouement they both took off to San Diego for a conference that had been planned months earlier, a get-together of management consultants who used the same time-and-motion system to measure how long such tasks as changing the oil in an engine or welding a certain length of steel should actually take. This was not their first trip to California, a few years earlier they had returned from one raving about the architecture in Santa Barbara, but it seemed to me that this would be a timely opportunity to clear the air. They returned to announce to all of us that Dad had accepted a job with Bob Nolan's company as Vice-President of a new division that would focus on manufacturing and they would be moving to Connecticut in a few weeks' time. They might as well have told us they were moving to Mars. And what about this unfinished ten- year business plan? But there was more. The two other key managers in our business, Peter, who ran production, and Aubrey, who had taken over my old sales role, also announced that they were leaving to set up their own business and had licensed some kind of vacuum moulding technology. Once again what was good for the goose was good for the gander. It was impossible to say who knew what when but I was entirely in the dark about all of this.

Mary and John now had two children, Rex, and his baby sister, Layla, who had been born on the winter solstice of nineteen eighty-two. John's building business had fallen victim to this unending recession and they would now move into our parents' house. There was no immediate plan to sell it as Finbarr was halfway through a civil engineering degree and Anne was still in school. As for Michael he was, so far as we knew, holding down a job as a computer programmer in London. Dad's short-lived foray into the computer business had allowed him to pluck Michael from a career of selling encyclopaedias and put him on a trajectory that would serve him well for the rest of his life. However, his main contribution to that company was to immediately start screwing the stunningly beautiful Trinity graduate teaching him programming. He became engaged to her briefly, then declared that anyone who would want to marry him had something wrong with them, broke it off, and left Ireland forever.

My future remained entirely based in Dublin, so in due course a couple of us loaded up the company van with our prototype car telephones and took a ferry to Liverpool, then drove to Manchester to a telecom trade show to tout our wares. Here we were exposed to an alarming new development. The Swedes had developed something called a cellular phone which did away with you having to erect an enormous antenna in your back garden. Moreover the range of your phone was only limited by the availability of antennas that could be shared by everyone with one of these phones. Devastated, we slunk back across the Irish Sea to come up with the next best thing.

No sooner was I home than the phone rang. It was Mary. "Sean, you had better come down here. Dad is closing down the company."

"What?"

"Yeah, he gave Peter and Aubrey a bunch of equipment and I heard them saying that the liquidators will be there to change the locks on Monday."

"So why would I drive down there?"

"Well, he's doing all this behind your back."

"So I confront him with being a liar? Do you think that will sway him?"

"I am just trying to help."

I hung up the dark green phone that sat atop a couple of phone books at the foot of the stairs. The floor itself was also darkish green. We had stained the floorboards and then varnished them. We could not yet afford carpet as the mortgage consumed well over half my take-home pay.

Mary was not trying to help me. She was revelling in this. She knew what was happening before I did. She could not resist the opportunity of being the one to tell me my whole life had just gone up in smoke. Michael and Mary hated me for my success and now that was all about to be undone. I had done all the work to rescue the company while they had done nothing. Lily had deliberately underpriced all the business in her last few months and it was only my master stroke in winning the Bombardier Bus wiring that had saved us.

It was always the same. No matter what I did right it was not good enough and no matter what they did wrong it was never bad enough for them to have any consequences. I went into the kitchen where a now very noticeably pregnant Kate was feeding Justin in his high chair. I let out an involuntary chortle.

"Well, on Monday I need to start looking for a job."

Kate herself was not working nor did either of us expect her to with Justin hardly a toddler yet and another baby on the way. This was a bitter blow though not entirely unexpected. The announcement of the parents' move to America had been a complete surprise but in the weeks that followed we had been left to speculate on their motivation. Were they seizing the opportunity to make a fortune across the pond or were they just running away from the steaming mess on their own doorstep? But , still, why not take off on a great adventure now that the youngest of the five of us had turned eighteen?

We mulled it over as Justin ate his banana, squeezing it into mush with his chubby fingers. He was a great eater and as solid as a bear cub. And now his Daddy had no job and would soon have no money to pay for food, clothes or heating oil, let alone the mortgage itself. Whatever their original intentions this latest act was obviously an act of retribution aimed squarely at me for my disloyalty. But who had I been disloyal to and was it right to lump both Mom and Dad together? She was as pure of heart as Desdemona while his was as black as that of Iago.

They had married each other in nineteen fifty-five, virgins, as I said earlier, and I had been a honeymoon baby, a wedding night baby for all I know. Ena had been put through teacher training but that left no funds to do anything similar for her younger sister. However, Doreen, equally as intelligent, sat the Civil Service exams, passed handily and went to work for the Department of Finance. That, of course, came to an abrupt end the day of her marriage. Married women were not allowed to work for the government. From that moment on she was entirely dependent on her husband for everything. All forms of contraception were illegal, even condoms, and the babies issued forth on a regular basis, in every family. Divorce had been outlawed as soon as my grandfather and his fellow revolutionaries sent the British packing and abortion was regarded as an unspeakable abomination.

She had no choice but to follow him for the rest of her life. One of her most frequent phrases when things were going badly for me was to tell me to "offer it all up," meaning that whatever suffering came your way would earn you a higher place in heaven. But as I had long shed my belief in an afterlife it was of little consequence to me where I might fit in it. Moreover, when I would ask for input on what to do when I left school she always redirected me to my father, saying that his education had only begun where hers had ended. But surely if Mary knew what Dad was up to Mom did too and if so how could she escape realizing the awful situation this was about to create for Kate, me, Justin and the new baby?

And what was the point of just flipping a switch and turning the lights out? The business had operated profitably ever since the first Bombardier bus rolled off the assembly line in Shannon. True, that business was now drying up and the hoped for orders for more buses from Iraq were supposedly just on hold until the latest war over there ended. We had certainly eviscerated the business with all these attempts at diversification but we were by no means dead in the water. Only now we were, and I with my twenty percent piece of paper was powerless to stop this. I was not nauseous at this news as I had been when I found out about Ena, I was just stunned, shocked, gobsmacked.

The next day, Saturday, I had Finbarr and my friend Bren meet me at the factory. We dismantled the conference room table and loaded it and its chairs into the delivery van. There wasn't much else worth taking. The computer was leased and anyway was too big to take and would be too hard to put to some new use before it was obsolete. It was eerie walking around the shop floor. I had literally created all this, including managing the construction of the building itself, my first task when I came to work for Lily, oblivious to her future machinations, let alone what was now unfolding. The heavy dark wood table looked great when we set it up in our dining room, although the bright red upholstery on the ultra-modern tubular steel chairs was, to say the least, unusual.

I don't know how they arranged it, but on Monday when I turned up in my gleaming white Peugeot with its precious sunroof, Peter and about a dozen workers were there finishing off the work in progress. I put on as brave a face as I could and climbed the stairs to where a couple of accountants had set themselves up. They had hauled a small work table into the space left vacant by the table I had stolen. There was an open milk carton on it and some of our coffee mugs and a teapot. I gave them the keys of the Peugeot and left. Kate was waiting for me in her little blue Mini, with Justin strapped into the back. We drove away and I never laid eyes on the place again.

Chapter Six. 1984.

Walk On Hot Coals
Rory Gallagher

Some events, sights or sounds, or even tastes and smells, are seared into our memories, while other whole tracts of time are impossible to recall with any accuracy. In the weeks that followed my parents did leave for America. I don't recall exactly when, but I knew exactly where they were going. The Nolans had now built a compound in the same town they had always lived in, Simsbury, Connecticut. It had a huge main house, a pool, a volleyball and/ or tennis court, and a guest house. I had stayed there several times, getting high as a kite, music blaring, with Dan Nolan, most recently when Kate and I went on our American honeymoon three years earlier. This was where they would stay while they got established.

Meanwhile, I had signed up with Ireland's pre-eminent executive headhunters who were very bullish on placing me, largely based on my industrial sales background. But the days dragged on and turned into weeks. I was now on the dole which at that time was dispensed from a building in Mountjoy Square. One in five people were jobless and this office was thronged all day every day. After five years blissfully out of step I had now joined their ranks. Some weeks I took Justin with me to give Kate a break, other times I went alone. On those occasions I was free to walk around the corner to a bar that had installed a VCR and a big telly. This filled the place up by lunchtime and the dole money and the pints flowed freely all day to whatever double-header was on. This movie rental business was still very new and the studios were still loathe to release recent movies to videotape as long as they had any other way to squeeze revenue from them.

I really didn't care what I was watching. I was feeling far too much anger to focus on the plot. I was angry at my mother for telling me over and over how great my father was and how he was just his own worst enemy. I was still livid at this huge betrayal but at the same time plagued with doubt as to the extent to which I had brought this on myself. Was this going to happen anyway once Dad no longer had both women fawning over him? After all, he had gone from who knew how many years of successful bigamy, patriarch of his clan, captain of industry, to having his wife find out what he was really like, to having his lover die right after this, of cancer, or shame, or both, to being exposed as a philandering bastard yet again by me.

The dole office was close to the centre of Dublin. I sat in that pub one morning drinking a pint of Guinness and smoking a Hamlet cigar, when a new thought bubbled to the surface. My whole life had been shaped by other people's dreams. My mother wanted the perfect family and as her oldest child I had to help make that happen, primarily by setting a very good example to the younger ones. My father was a a control freak. Every time I went to him for career advice it came back to engineering. Medicine took too long. I wasn't artistic enough to be an architect. You could always be a pilot after you became an engineer. And what could you do with a degree in English except teach or be a bloody journalist?

And there it was. The only subject I really enjoyed in school was English. Oh, I was good at everything, but I relished English class. I liked reading *King Lear*. I found Oscar Wilde hilarious. I memorized lines out of *Wuthering Heights*. I even enjoyed translating the short stories of Guy De Maupassant from French into English, just as I enjoyed short stories in general. As a teenager I wrote poetry, lots of it. I taught myself how to write a sonnet. And I read voraciously. I wasn't so much drawn to high-brow literature as to genres like science fiction, fantasy, and adventure stories. I had read every Alistair MacLean novel and I had discovered Michael Crichton. Why had I not thought of this before? I stubbed out the cigar and left.

Mountjoy Square was a part of Georgian Dublin that had seen better days. Entire buildings in the facades had collapsed and their neighbours were now propped up with huge lean-to timbers. The entire North Side was dreary and dilapidated, but it was a short walk to the top of O'Connell Street, and from there down our widest boulevard past the General Post Office to the country's largest bookstore, Easons. The entire ground floor was devoted to newspapers, magazines and a display of the latest hardbacks. You had to take the escalator to the second floor to reach the enormous assortment of paperbacks. And then I had to take another set of stairs to the third floor to find the less sought-after self-help and how-to-do-it books. There were only two books that claimed to tell you how to write a novel so I bought both of them.

Back home I eagerly devoured what these books had to teach me. The first was a breezy memoir written by an English novelist who I had never heard of. It did have practical advice about the writing life and cautioned me to write about things I knew. The other book concerned itself mainly with point of view, with lots of examples. I could write in the first person, as I am here, but then the reader can only see or know what I see or know. I now learned that most novels are written in the third person either as single or multiple viewpoint or omniscient narrator. This was all very helpful but it still left me with absolutely no idea what I could or should write about.

The days were getting longer, the crocuses and the daffodils and the tulips had all come and gone. One sunny day we piled into the Mini and drove down to Naas to see Kate's parents. We now knew we were going to have a baby daughter, so, as we had agreed, if it was a girl I would get to name her. Kate had chosen the very classical name, Justin, and given him the middle name, Michael, in honour of her only brother, and certainly not my flaky sibling. The little girl next door to us was named Saoirse, the Irish word for freedom, which I thought was awesome. Having shown Justin off for a couple of hours we drove out to my old home where we found Mary with her two kids, Rex and Layla.

There were empty beer bottles, a couple of mugs, and a full ashtray on the back table in the atrium. Mary was sitting in this big open room so that Rex could toddle around as there was nothing he could pull at or get into here. Kate lowered herself slowly into a chair and Mary lit a cigarette. John came in from the dining room where he had been studying and joined us.

"Any luck on the job front?" John asked.

"Nope, but I get a phone call every other week from the recruiter," I replied.

"Yeah, this bloke who's our instructor keeps reminding us there are eight hundred computer programmers out of work but as I keep telling him I'll take my chances. There are forty-thousand building workers on the dole."

"How are you keeping up with your mortgage and all that? Mary asked.

I was tempted to tell her we were going to be evicted next week to see her reaction, but instead I told her the truth.

"I met with the building society and they've given us a moratorium."

Mary and Kate started a conversation about the kids while John rolled his own cigarette. I walked into the dining room and closed the door to keep Rex from coming in. The outer wall had a huge window facing onto Gillespie's field where we often watched the cattle coming and going from the milking parlour. The opposite wall had a fireplace in the middle with floor-to-ceiling shelving on either side of it. The left-hand shelves held some china and silver but the right hand one had books jammed into it anywhere they would fit. I began reading their spines. They were all paperbacks of varying heights and thicknesses. I had read some of them, but I had no interest in Joan Collins and had read Wilbur Smith and most of the others. *The Year of The French* had been made into a TV series, an unusual undertaking by our always cash-strapped national station. *The Great Hunger* was too depressing to read.

And then I noticed the white writing on the black spine. *The Táin*, translated by Thomas Kinsella. I pulled it out. Brush illustrations by Louis Le Brocquy. I did not know who either of these people were but I knew what this book was about. It was about Cuchulainn, Ireland's most famous mythological hero. There was a huge bronze statue of him in the General Post Office. We learned a smattering of Irish myths and fairy tales in school, in both Irish and English. *The Children Of Lír, Finn McCool, Deirdre Of The Sorrows,* and the poem, *The Faeries.*

Up the airy mountain
Down the rushy glen
We daren't go a hunting
For fear of little men

You could never get that out of your head. At some point along the way I had read The Táin. It even had a map. It told the story of a war fought between the rulers of two of Ireland's four provinces, Maeve, high-queen of Connacht, and Conor MacNessa, high-king of Ulster. I had forgotten about the map, which leant the possibility that this had been an actual event. Was there something here?

I went into the living room with its sunken red carpet. This too had some built in shelving to the left of the fireplace. The waist-high top shelf held the stereo and below it there was a shelf of vinyl records, including some boxed sets of classical music that no-one ever listened to. Below this the bottom shelf was filled with hardback books, including all of the old Time-Life ones Dad had subscribed to many years ago. To the right of these I found what I was looking for. It was a thick hardback volume just called *The Celts*. I picked it up. The first word of each chapter began with an enormous pretentious letter like you would find in *The Book Of Kells*. I found a second book on Celtic Art and left with all three books.

"Rex has a bad cough again," said Kate as we drove away. "I hope he hasn't given it to Justin, or the baby. And I don't want to be around any more smokers before I give birth or to have Justin or our baby inhaling secondhand smoke either."

I was only half listening. I was planning my next trip to Easons. They carried Lady Gregory's *Cuchulainn Of Muirthemne* and her other book *Gods And Mortal Men*. I needed both of them along with a couple of notebooks. When we had developed the car telephone we had, of course, applied for an R&D grant. We got it with the stipulation that we use the University of Limerick's new radio frequency lab to validate our design. I got to know the lecturer in charge and on one visit he pointed to an Apple II in the corner and asked me if we had a use for it. I looked it over. It was the latest iteration. There was the computer itself with a sloping front that held the keyboard. On top sat a square metal box that was the monitor and on the right were two floppy disk drives, connected via two grey ribbon cables that we had made in our factory. Apple gave us lots of volume, terrible prices, but paid really fast.

The trip to Limerick in the Mini took all day with the usual traffic snarl going through Portlaoise, but now I had something a lot better than a typewriter and on the way back I stopped into Mary and John's again, went down to the now disused offices, found a dot matrix printer and even a full box of tractor drive paper. By the time I arrived home I was already homing in on the point of view I would use for my story. I had pages and pages of family tree diagrams, some from the real mythology and some that I had made up myself.

Two of my favourite authors were J.R.R Tolkien and Mary Renault. I had long since read *The Hobbit* and more recently *The Lord Of The Rings*, which I read twice, mainly because I had bought the middle volume, *The Twin Towers*, without realizing that was what it was, so I read all the way to the end, then turned around and read the whole thing again. Mary Renault was a South African novelist, a Lesbian nurse as it happens, who never set foot in Greece, but whose most famous work is a trilogy on the life of Alexander The Great. Again, I had read them out of sequence, picking up a copy of *The Persian Boy,* then *Funeral Games* and then *Fire From Heaven.* Together they provided me with all kinds of descriptions of ancient warfare.

I set myself up on the stolen conference room table in the dining room and started typing. It was slow going at first, but after a couple of weeks I had one complete chapter. Since Kate was there and spent a lot of time resting she was a willing reader and seemed to follow what I was writing. That one chapter, in book form thirty pages of prose, was more than I had ever written before in my entire life. Cuchulainn, literally Culann's hound, though more usually the hound of Ulster, had the given name Setanta, which he would have been called by his friends, but he was not the protagonist of my story. I had come up with a much more tragic approach - I would make the doomed Ferdia my hero.

And on and on I went, recreating the ancient city of Emain, positioning Ferdia as a chariot racer, and introducing an ever-widening circle of characters, including the sons of Uisliu, that would enable me to embrace the entire Deirdre of The Sorrows sub-plot and create a schism that would drive Ferdia to flee to Connacht and fight on their side in the coming war. I was completely immersed in this imagined world. This was the happiest I had been in a long, long time. I didn't want it to end other than with the publication to great acclaim of my epic novel. The headhunter continued to call with his usual exhortations not to worry, keep my spirits up, and don't lose hope. But now he was just another interloper from the unwanted and pointless outside world.

On June twenty-first, nineteen eighty-four, the longest day of the year, the summer solstice, Kate gave birth to our baby daughter. I had decided to call her Aisling Helen, but at the last minute, in deference to the fact that we had given our son the classical name, Justin, I reversed this and we named her Helen Aisling, Helen after Helen of Troy, since we knew we made her in Greece, and Aisling, being the Irish word for beautiful vision. It was an auspicious birthday and she would grow up to be one of the happiest, sunniest children I have ever met.

I continued writing but now I began to have new doubts. Was this fair to my wife and children? I had gone down the path of having a family in the full expectation of being able to provide us with a standard of living similar to or better than what I myself had experienced. By now my interest in the writing business had made me aware that most writers did not make a viable living. Mario Puzo had lived with his parents for years while writing The Godfather, because he had to. James Joyce was propped up by a circle of admirers and patrons. Gregory, Yeats and Synge were landed gentry. For God's sake, Mozart was buried in a pauper's grave and Van Gogh never sold a painting.

How long would it take to write this? How would you even go about finding a publisher? So far as I could tell there were only three Irish publishers of fiction: O'Brien Press, Wolfhound Press, and Mercier Press down in Cork. This process could take years with no guarantee of success. But just as I had been a slave to the family business for those six years I might as well keep going with this until some gainful employment somehow presented itself. This more somber mood was actually helpful because I had reached a point where I needed to flesh out the Ulster high-king as a treacherous bastard. Besides, there was less free time now.

Justin was not yet toilet-trained and Kate was breast-feeding Helen. We now realized that having one child was a dawdle, but two small babies was a full-time job for both of us. And Justin was a bundle of energy. The last time I had been on the phone he had gotten away from me, climbed the stairs and flung himself back down. Fortunately I was there to break his fall and stop him from gashing his head open on the radiator. There was at least that. Kate did not have to manage both of them on her own.

The days of course grew shorter ever since Helen's birth. It was the middle of August and I was on chapter eight when the phone rang. It was my ever-friendly head-hunter.

"Sean, something has come up that might be a good fit. They're an American multi-national based in Cork. They make electronic components and they are looking for a sales manager for Ireland. It sounds really up your alley."

"Fantastic. What do I do?"

"Their HR Manager wants to meet you tomorrow in The Intercontinental at two p.m. His name is Jack Slyne and he will be waiting for you at reception. Bring your C.V."

Chapter Seven. 1984 - 1985.

Whether 'tis nobler in the mind to suffer
The slings and arrows of outrageous fortune,
Or to take arms against a sea of troubles
And by opposing end them.

Hamlet
Act III, Scene 1, lines 59-62
William Shakespeare

The company's name was Bourns Electronics Inc and their headquarters was in Riverside, California. They made a variety of electronic components in factories all over the world. They were in the process of doubling the size of their Irish operation which, like most of the other multi-nationals who had set up shop there, existed to supply the European market. After a cursory look at my resume, Slyne ordered me to take a train to Cork the following week, where I was interviewed in a lot more depth by John Sheehan, the Managing Director, to whom I would report.

They sent a job offer the following week and Sheehan's secretary booked a flight to Cork for both Kate and I to have a look around. By this time Kate's sister was living with us so Kate just had to leave her with enough breast milk for the day. I was no stranger to Cork and already had a fairly good idea of what I wanted to do. First of all, this was a field sales job so I would be buzzing around the country a lot of the time, so no need to be in the factory all the time. Secondly, we could not buy a house here until we sold the one in Dublin, and there was now an enormous glut of homes on the market, dropping in value every day, so we would have to rent for a while. And finally, Cork was a port city with lots of coastal villages within easy driving distance.

We rented a house in Kinsale, a small fishing village nestled into the last sharp bend in the Bandon River before it widens out and meets The Atlantic Ocean. It is unlike any other town in Ireland, a perfect anchorage for yachts of all sizes, with a maze of narrow streets going back hundreds of years, a jumble of maritime architecture with influences from all over Europe, and a plethora of ancient bars and gourmet restaurants. It oozed history and adventure, with Charles Fort looming over the eastern cliffs and James Fort facing the town from the promontory that forced the river to change direction.

It took a few weeks to get Kate and the kids moved and settled in the long bungalow facing the harbour. You could see all the moored boats and tell whether the tide was rising or falling by the direction they all pointed. If you went out our gate and turned left you could take the cliff path all the way to Charles Fort, turning right took you around the harbour and into town. We literally lived in a postcard, a photo of Kinsale taken from across The Bandon, showing the harbour, the yachts at their moorings, small trawlers tethered to the pier, and layers of stone and slate buildings rising up the hill into the distance. And there was our rented bungalow perched above the lane that ran all the way along the edge of the estuary. You could buy this postcard anywhere postcards were sold. And we now had two cars again, Kate's Mini and my new silver Toyota Carina. Kinsale was also the gateway to West Cork with its legendary beaches and seaside towns, Courtmacsherry, Clonakilty, Baltimore, Schull, Crookhaven and Bantry.

Kate found a day care for Justin and began frequenting Patsy's Corner, the local coffee shop. Friends were eager to visit us and marvelled at the local scene. There were hoi-paloi hotels called The Trident, Acton's, and The Blue Haven. There was a shack by the pier that sold fish and chips and called itself The Lusitania Grill. There was The Greyhound Bar right in the middle with its three tiny rooms warmed by coal fires. There was The White Lady, a late-night joint run by an Englishman who would make you a steak cooked over a grate that he fanned with a hairdryer. The Spaniard just up the hill from our house had music most weekends. You could stop at The Bulman for a pint on the way to the fort and listen to the actual Bulman clanging away in the harbour.

There was endless entertainment and stimulation. As the winter rolled in we got to know more and more of the locals, the chefs, bartenders, artists, and writers. Kate met a mother her own age in Patsy's, Bernadette Crowley, and she turned out to be married to Mary Black's piano player and played a mean fiddle herself. She took water samples incessantly, convinced that the Pfizer factory was polluting the water supply and that men were starting to grow breasts. She persuaded Kate to join the local opera society and they rehearsed Gilbert and Sullivan's Pirates of Penzance every week for months and months. Kate started taking windsurfing lessons.

I bought myself a pair of binoculars and took up bird-watching. After a hard Saturday night Kate liked to lie in, so I took Justin and Helen with me to all the muddy tidal estuaries that filled up with migrating birds in winter. They were both still in diapers so there was a bit of planning involved. I just loved the stillness and would find a vantage point that had the low winter sun behind me, lighting up the curlews, godwits and oystercatchers, the ever-present seagulls, and the occasional heron or cormorant. Dublin was all of a hundred and eighty miles away, but this was a different world. Perhaps I was yet again out of step with society at large but here I relished the experience.

Although I was now extremely focused on this new job I had not entirely given up on my writing project. I was learning all about birds to improve my descriptions in my half-finished war novel. I realized I had no idea what kinds of plants and animals made up the Ireland of two thousand years earlier. For instance, I had read that chestnut trees were introduced to Britain by the Romans, so there would not have been any here. And although there would have been grassy meadows you could probably have walked the length of the country under cover of a deciduous forest.

Not only were we making social progress in Kinsale, but I was getting to know my colleagues at work. Most of them were Cork natives, which was the whole point of setting up these factories all over Ireland, but a few, like me, were not. Gerry O'Connor, head of finance, was not. His wife, Anne, was also a nurse and she and Kate hit it off immediately. We got together for New Year's Eve and ushered in nineteen eighty-five with dinner at Man Friday's near our house and then we crashed the celebrations at Acton's Hotel.

Michael was still in England and there were rumours of a girlfriend. Mary was not working but John had picked up a good job in the new information technology field while she stayed at home to mind Rex and now two-year-old Layla. Finbarr studied on and Anne, now finished school, was pursuing some journalism course. They all still lived together in the house in Kildare. Everyone, of course, had an open invitation to come and visit, but so far there were no takers. I have no idea what my parents did that Christmas.

Life was good for us, but the economy as a whole was not improving. Even though all we were asking for our house in Dublin was a price that would clear the mortgage there were no offers. But so far there was also no sign that the building society would foreclose on us. It was a worry, but sleeping in our big waterbed with the curtains open, looking out over the harbour, with the jingling of the halliards wafting across the water, like a symphony of bells, more than made up for it. The days grew longer and we finally toilet-trained Justin. Daffodils and wild garlic and pink lilac sprouted in the rocky slope behind our house while across the harbour yellow gorse and red fuchsia lit up James Fort.

My sales job was now more or less in autopilot when suddenly the Manufacturing Manager had an altercation with John Sheehan and stormed out. I asked for his job and got it. Now I went from having a part-time assistant to having three hundred workers and I went from interfacing with the UK sales office and the Swiss sales headquarters to being a part of the worldwide manufacturing operations and exchanging emails and phone calls every day with various functional heads at the California headquarters. And we were busy with several automation projects, grant-aided of course, to keep Ireland competitive with Mexico and Costa Rica. I was suddenly very relevant.

We went on another trip to Greece that summer with our friends, this time to Rhodes and a few smaller islands. Kate arranged to leave Justin with her mother and Mary said she would mind Helen. We were not too sure about this but we couldn't leave both kids with the grandmother and Mary was a stay-at-home mother with her own two. Our doubts were well-founded. Kate did an excellent job keeping Justin and Helen in great health, always clean, and always dressed in freshly laundered clothes. What we came back to shocked us. Our baby daughter's bottom was covered in bleeding sores.

We were more furious at ourselves than at Mary. We knew she neglected her own children but just did not think that you could get to such a state in two weeks. Neither of our kids had ever had nappy rash. Helen even had a runny nose, presumably infected by being around ever-snotty Rex and Layla. Even MotherKenny, our chain-smoking, Guinness-drinking, paternal grandmother began to comment on the comparison. Justin and Helen were clearly the product of the very best motherly care, while Rex and Layla were unkempt ragamuffins.

It was hard to tell whether Mary was just oblivious to this or, since none of her peers had any kids yet, just thought this was normal. In fact we saw very little of the rest of the family after we moved away from Dublin so it was not as if the comparison was in her face often. And her own mother was on the other side of the Atlantic in no position to chime in or give advice. We went about the task of healing our baby and soon she was back to her old self, waking up in her cot singing to herself, waiting patiently for us to come and get her. She never had any kind of rash ever again.

The house finally sold but we continued to rent. Idyllic though Kinsale was, the Irish economy showed no signs of improving. In fact, the population at large was now so depressed people in large numbers began to see apparitions of moving statues of The Virgin Mary. The most popular of these was a few miles outside of Kinsale in the tiny village of Ballinspittle. We went to investigate this ourselves and found a typical plaster madonna set in an alcove beneath an ivy-covered hillside. In order to light up the cave and add a more heavenly aura a halo of lights had been installed over the statue. This was supported by a single hard-to-see post behind the head of the statue. Naturally, when the wind blew, this ring of lights did actually move back and forth slightly. This in turn caused the shadows to flicker and gave the illusion of movement. Thousands flocked to see this, jamming up the roads and pubs every weekend.

Back at work events took yet another unexpected twist. The doubling of the size of the factory was now complete and John Sheehan fully expected to be Managing Director of all of it, but the Americans had other ideas. Two different business units now operated side by side, and they reported into two completely separate management structures. The new business unit wanted their own factory manager reporting into their headquarters in Utah. Sheehan was enraged. He quickly found another job and resigned.

By this time I had met all of the top management of the business unit whose products I made. I would always volunteer to pick them up at Cork Airport, take them to and from their hotel, have dinner with them, and wait with them at the airport for their departing flight. And it paid off. They had no hesitation in giving me John Sheehan's old job, which came with his office, his secretary, and his car, a big Ford Granada. I was now one of seven global plant managers, reporting directly to the Vice-President of Operations in Riverside, California. All was now most well with the world.

The days grew shorter, the tourists fewer, and Mom and Dad announced they were coming to Ireland for Christmas. I was to pick them up from Shannon Airport, which meant driving cross-country the day before and staying at a local hotel. I brought now toilet-trained and much more manageable Justin with me and put him to bed, then went back down to the bar and drank up a storm. I was dreading this confrontation and made it all the worse by sleeping in and being hours late to meet them. Dad ignored me, buried in The Irish Times, but Mom gushed over Justin and then went into her best conciliation mode saying let's all just enjoy ourselves and a reticent Dad was left with no choice but to comply and we all piled into the big Granada and I retraced the route to Kinsale.

Baby Helen, who they had not yet met, trumped all animosity, and we settled into a cordial visit. Kinsale held magical memories for them even more than for us. We visited Charles Fort where Dad reminded me of putting Michael and I into a stone cell with a sheer drop into the ocean when we were very young boys. I had not forgotten that tour, at a time when the locals, as they do in every impoverished corner of the world, coerced you into employing a guide. I even remembered much of what he had said, about Cromwell using the local church to stable his horses, and about the lightning flashes that had lit up the spears of the approaching Irish trying to rendezvous with the Spanish at the Battle of Kinsale, wrecking their surprise tactic, and the unmarked graves of the victims of The Lusitania, torpedoed and sunk by the Huns off Old Head, in that same church.

"What would you like to do tomorrow?" I asked.

"How far are we from Ballinspittle?" asked my mother.

They had heard of this all the way on the other side of the pond.

"A few miles."

I took both of them there next day.

"I definitely see that statue moving," said Dad.

"Oh yes," chimed in Mom. "Do you not see it, Sean?"

"The statue is not moving. That is not possible"

"What? Oh, God, no. I saw it," said Dad.

"You didn't. It's a trick of the light."

"Why are you so cynical?" Mom asked.

"You brought me up to believe in science, in evolution, to play chess, and then you sent me to engineering school. This is superstitious nonsense"

"Oh no," said Dad, "I saw it move."

I drove them back to the house where they regaled Kate, busy feeding the kids, with how they had seen the statue move with their own eyes. They tried to pull her into the argument. They failed and we lit a coal fire, put Helen to bed, and read stories to Justin for a while. Dad went into a long monologue about how all the other Nolan consultants would fly anywhere just to have a meeting with a prospective client. Neither of them asked about my job or congratulated me on my rapid progress. It was as if they themselves were responsible for this recent success and had somehow planned this all along. It was not me who had dug my own little family out of the hole they had created, but them. The gratitude trap was sprung yet again.

Chapter Eight. 1985 - 1987.

"Men's courses will foreshadow certain ends,
*   to which, if persevered in, they must lead," said Scrooge. "But if the courses*
be departed from, the ends will change."

A Christmas Carol
Charles Dickens

On Christmas Eve the six of us piled into the Granada and drove north for six hours through the rich farmlands of Munster and then the entire length of Connacht with its bogs and lakes until we reached Ballina and turned west for another half hour, pointing out the stone walls running up to the tops of un-arable hills, a legacy of The Great Famine, to reach our destination, a small development of holiday homes near the village of Ballycastle. We had rented two of these for this family get-together. With the exception of Michael the rest of the family were already there, including MotherKenny.

John and Mary were working on the turkey. It had slipped down through a hole in the floor of their rusty jalopy and picked up a coating of stones. We unloaded the groceries we had brought and made a pot of tea. It didn't feel very Christmassy. There was no tree and no decorations and although we had some nicely wrapped presents we would not put those out until the kids went to bed. On top of that there was no Christmas cake, an enterprise that took months to prepare what with baking and almond icing and royal icing and little ornaments, nor was there any Christmas pudding, MotherKenny being long past organizing the ingredients and boiling it up weeks in advance. None of the younger women had any interest in learning to make these Victorian staples, so this would just be the turkey, stuffing, and vegetables.

We had forgotten about Michael, who we were supposed to meet off the train in Ballina, but he had put himself in a taxi and walked in the door, three sheets to the wind, and the reunion was now complete. The four children went down for the night and I set about putting together a tricycle for Justin, while John oiled up the secondhand one he had bought Rex, and added a shiny mirror to make it look new. We sent Finbarr to look for an off license and he returned with a few six-packs. Michael, Mary, John, Finbarr, and

60

Anne all smoked, so the room grew hazy as we caught up on each others' goings on. Mom and Dad already had green cards and were going to become citizens as soon as possible. Mom was learning to ski. John was excited about his new programming job. Finbarr had spent a year in America but was now back living with MotherKenny with a view to finishing his degree. Anne had a job with a small newspaper. We couldn't get a straight answer out of Michael as to what exactly he was doing.

Christmas morning was all about the little kids. We bundled up the two boys against the freezing wind and took them up and down the road on their trikes. The women bustled around in the kitchen, and some of us played a game of Monopoly while the turkey was roasting. A Fawlty Towers marathon was playing on the television and Dad sat in an armchair guffawing from time to time but otherwise disengaged. The world no longer revolved around him and he clearly didn't like it. This was not his house today and he could not take control of what went on in it, so he just ignored it all.

On Stephen's Day we hiked up DownPatrick Head with the wind howling to the point that conversation was impossible. I wondered if I was being too harsh in my judgment. But I couldn't shake it off. Dad had lied to me all those years ago in order to enveigle me into a situation that was itself a nest of lies. And then when I had done all that was asked of me he had betrayed me yet again. But maybe he had done the right thing by making a fresh start in America and leaving all of the bad memories behind. They were already talking up how to bring at least Finbarr and Anne over. They were buying a house and moving out of the Nolan guest house. Who was I to throw cold water on it all?

Though I was only vaguely aware of it, in truth the magic circle was now broken. All five of us were independent adults. Our parents, in their own ways, had done their best to raise us. And there it was, I finally grasped it. I was dealing with three separate relationships. There was my cruel and at times sadistic father. Who terrified two small boys by pretending he was going to reverse the Volkswagen off the quay into the river Liffey on Sunday mornings? Who laughed before slapping two small boys on the backs of their legs for talking at Mass because we were already crying knowing what was coming? And who would then banish those same boys to the garage to sit on the frame of a boat trailer bawling while the adults conversed around the dining room table? And once, when my hayfever was acting up and I was wheezing he told me to stop breathing if I couldn't breathe without making noise.

Then there was my mother, always kind, always encouraging, but never willing to stand up to him. Instead, she looked to me to fill that emotional void, to be an example to my siblings and help her raise them. She always saw the best in people, with a handful of exceptions. And finally there was "them", my two parents as a single item, amplified by Mom telling us all how great Dad really was, how he worked so hard because he loved us all so much, and how we didn't know how good we had it. And now here "they" were, in lock-step again, setting up home in the New World and enticing at least their three unwed children to come and join them.

We left this place of which Oliver Cromwell once said there wasn't a tree tall enough to hang a man, nor water deep enough to drown him, nor soil enough to then bury him. A strange place for this rendezvous, with its famine walls and famine harbours, full of the ghosts of a time when it had been considered a Congested District, devoid of people now. It was the last time we would all be together for Christmas and we all parted on the best of terms. Back in Kinsale, Kate and I began to mull over our own options. I had only recently been promoted and was still in the midst of a project to replace most of the workforce with assembly automation from Italy, the USA, and Switzerland. I would have to see all of that through to success before I could realistically campaign to move to America with this company. But Kate was a registered nurse and those were in high demand in the USA and there was a fast track to entry. She would have to sit an exam called the CGFNS, and also demonstrate experience across a range of specialties. She had worked cardiac and ICU but they also wanted psychiatric, which she didn't have.

Kate and Anne O'Connor were now volunteer nurses at the Cork Family Planning Clinic. There were now a few of these around the country established by progressive medical professionals as a way to circumvent Ireland's draconian ban on any form of contraception. If a doctor prescribed the pill or an IUD then no politician or cleric would have the balls to go up against that lest he be blamed for some fatal miscarriage. In reality half of what they did was provide sex education to clueless women who literally didn't know where babies came from. So all Kate had to do was to ask around to find that, yes, there was a lunatic asylum in Cork City and, yes, they would absolutely love to have her as a volunteer nurse there. They set her to work in an observation station with unbreakable glass windows and gave her a stack of case files to review. The inmates duly hurled both the furniture and themselves at the glass while Kate read about people who had been locked up in henhouses for decades on remote farms in the Cork and Kerry mountains.

Michael came to visit with his new English girlfriend, Jackie, who was very much a Saxon beauty with a page-boy hairstyle and almond-shaped hazel eyes. Jackie was also in the medical field. She was a radiographer. She was a unique visitor, routinely wandering the house after her morning shower wearing only a towel wrapped around her head. I was not sure what the point of this visit was. Michael and I had long since ceased to socialize. Our strained relationship came to a head one night after he had brought one of the new personal computers to the sailing club to calculate which boat had won in a series of Portsmouth Yardstick races in which all the members raced each other in a variety of sailing dinghies of different speeds and sizes. It took a ridiculously long time to come up with the results and pissed everybody off. We stopped off at Poulaphouca House on the way home and got seriously drunk. Then when we did get home Michael decided to assault Finbarr for some reason. I intervened and Michael swung at me. He missed and I flattened him with a left hook but I broke my ring-finger metacarpal and to this day my knuckles don't line up correctly.

Did he come here with Jackie to show her off to me? Or was it the other way round? Did he want to show off his family to her? If so we were his only option without flying across the pond since Mary and John were now camped out in one squalid rental after another back in Dublin. And, of course, a first-time English visitor was going to be far more impressed with West Cork than suburban Dublin. We really liked Jackie and felt she would be good for Michael. They left and we turned our attention once again to some strange ailments Kate had been experiencing. First, she had been developing an occasional limp when walking back from town, and now she was complaining of stomach pain. She vowed to see a doctor.

At work things took yet another dramatic turn. Guy Forney, the head of my business unit, and my boss's boss, and Bing Harding, the head of the other business unit and Doug Kelleher's boss's boss showed up unannounced with a third unknown American in tow. They had come to reorganize the Irish operation. Two completely separate management teams were all very well in theory, but it had led to total duplication. Doug and I both had seven managers under us which meant a total of sixteen company cars lined up in front of the building and that had not gone unnoticed. The management team was merged and half of the line managers were let go.

That, of course, created another predicament. Doug and I could not both be in charge of this. But before we could even speculate on that outcome, we were both taken aside and told that they did not want to lose either of us, so they were not giving either of us the top job, and that is why they had brought back Don Dressel from retirement, someone neither of us had ever heard of, and were putting him in charge for now. Doug would now run all of manufacturing and I would run all of engineering and materials. I now knew how John Sheehan had felt.

I fumed in a one on one with Forney but he just started filing his nails. He assured me that they thought very highly of me and did not want me to leave.

"You know," I told him, "in the back of my mind when I went looking for a job with a multi-national I hoped at some point it might lead to a job in the States."

Forney perked up at this and nodded his head. "That makes a lot of sense," he said, "then maybe you could contribute on a much wider basis."

"My wife is a nurse and we had been working on using that to get a work permit" I added.

In other words, the part I can't say out loud is now that you have shafted me and I have nothing to lose you either come up with something or I am out of here anyway.

"Isn't Box coming over here soon?" asked Forney.

I looked at a calendar. He would be in Züg, our Swiss sales HQ, then the plant in Scotland, then here in three weeks' time.

"Just make sure he's on board," Forney continued, then put his notepad into his thin valise, empty other than a plane ticket and passport, snapped it shut, and stood up.

"I'll run you to the airport."

"Nah, Bing and I will take a taxi."

Richard Box, VP of Operations, had been my boss for my brief tenure as Plant Manager. But he had been a party to all the automation projects for years before that. On his previous visit we had traveled to Bologna to review the progress of our machine and an identical one he had ordered for the Puerto Rico factory. I had been to California for the first time to a Plant Manager conference he had convened. I had been surprised by how many palm trees there were and I had stayed over for an extra day to visit Universal Studios. He was a gregarious, somewhat academic character with an inexhaustible retinue of aphorisms. Where Forney was crisp and decisive you never knew what Box was really thinking or which way he might turn, so this visit would have to be really well managed.

As usual I went to the airport only to find that Box had brought his wife, Susan, with him. This was unheard of and added a whole new entertainment challenge. She was a really warm vivacious person and they both explained that they had just been to see their son who was studying abroad in Barcelona. And, yes, this was Susan's first trip to Ireland. No, there was no need for me stay to dinner at the hotel. I asked about Susan's plans for the next day. She planned to just take a walk around Cork city.

"Here's a suggestion," I said as I unloaded their luggage. "I'll pick up Richard in the morning, but why don't I have my wife, Kate, come and get you, Susan, say around ten, take you for a tour around the coast, then we could all meet up in Kinsale after work. It stays light really late here in summer, so I could book a guided walking tour, and then we could go to dinner. It's got some great restaurants."

There was instant agreement to this, but there was consternation when I got home. Not only would Kate have to drive this American lady around in her tiny Mini, she would have to take both of the kids because there was no way she could guarantee they would be back before daycare closed and was unsure she could find a babysitter for later either. I told her this was just too important and she would have to make it work and went off to the Greyhound Bar, the usual haunt of the fellow who did the walking tours. Mercifully he was there and he was available at six next day.

There was no way to make contact with people who were driving around in those days and so I spent the entire next day fretting about how this might be going. On top of that, I had forgotten that there were a couple of American engineers in town and they would also have to be included in all of this. We were now a party of six and when I called Man Friday for a reservation they said they could only seat us around ten pm. I booked it anyway. The hotel restaurants were out of the question for the Boxes who would see them as little better than cafeterias. Blue Haven was good but inconsistent and anyway booked up when I called and The White Lady was known to serve out of date supermarket wine and God knows what the menu would be.

We had pre-arranged to meet at the two centuries old Lord Kingsale pub. It was unusually warm for an Irish summer day and while this half-timbered shebeen might be a cosy fire-lit tavern in winter, in this heat and with no ventilation it stank of smoke and stale beer. We ordered one obligatory round as we waited for our guide who duly arrived in a tweed cap and Wellington boots. We followed him down a couple of narrow streets to the old Protestant church.

"Your children are adorable," said Susan Box as we walked.

This was a huge relief to hear as I had not had an opportunity to get Kate out of earshot of the others and grill her on how the day had gone.

The guide took us around the side of the church and pointed out graves of unknown Lusitania victims, then picked up some oyster shells and talked about them, but I wasn't listening, I was intent on the faces of the Americans. They couldn't understand a word he was saying in his thick singsong Cork accent. We left the church and walked around a few corners to the remains of the old walls and they tried to decipher his history lesson about the Battle Of Kinsale and how the spears of the Irish had been lit up by lightning and gave away their positions and how we would all be speaking Spanish now were it not for that. Then we traipsed to the old market building for more balderdash about the English and cutting down all the trees, and then I gave him a few quid from my wallet and realized it was only seven-thirty.

Man Friday sat on a bluff near where we lived. We set out to walk around the stone quay and up the hill toward it. Richard Box and I were still in business attire and you could tell he was not a person who got much exercise. Sweat rolled off him, but he kept up a banter with us younger men, and I chimed in with a translation of the tour from low Corkonian to high Dublinese, an English dialect they all could understand. We reached

Man Friday a little after eight. No, they still could not seat us until ten as per our reservation. I led the merry group another few yards up the hill to The Spaniard pub where at least the views were superb and we could all sit outside. My heart was pounding, and not from the hike. I apologized profusely knowing they were all hungry to be reassured by the Boxes that no-one in Spain ate before ten anyway. And it was indeed another two eternally long hours before we were looking at our menus.

Fifteen months later Kate and I lined up with a hundred others outside the American Embassy in Dublin and waited for hours in the rain, my arm numb from holding the umbrella, and finally handed our Irish passports to the immigration officer who stamped them with a full page blue and red L1 visa for me and L2 visa for Kate. I could work he explained but she could not, which didn't matter because she already had her nursing work permit.

Chapter Nine. 1987-1991.

◇ They're coming to America

Got a dream to take them there
They're coming to America

Got a dream they've come to share ◇

Neil Diamond

The first thing we learned on arrival in Southern California is that small children just do not do well with jet lag. Every day Justin and Helen fell asleep with their heads on the table when we took them out for dinner. They were now five and three and would have no memories of Ireland in the years to come. Various conversations had made us aware that we had to be careful where we chose to live as the quality of schooling varied enormously from one school district to another. We settled on the town of Redlands, one town over from Riverside where I worked, and began looking at houses.

We found a house we really liked and could afford but there was the complication of my being an indentured servant to my employer. However we found a workaround for this and soon unloaded the couches that had been a wedding present from Mom and Dad and the old waterbed and the few other pieces we had brought with us into a brand new house that had been an orange grove a couple of years earlier. It had a tiled kitchen, a built-in microwave, and the development shared an outdoor swimming pool. The fronts of all the houses were fully landscaped and you were not allowed to alter that. There were no walls between the houses though the back gardens were fenced in plots of dirt that you could do with as you liked.

I was now Richard Box's Staff Assistant, tasked with all kinds of special projects. I organized an automation conference. I headed up a task force on solderability. In reality I was a spare Plant Manager and the expectation was that I would take over the facility in Ames, Iowa, as that individual was expected to retire soon. But for now we set our minds on exploring this amazing new world. I bought a Chevy Blazer, a new kind of vehicle called an SUV, which was halfway between a car and a truck. I bought a big, thick travel guide to Southern California, a tent, four sleeping bags, a Coleman camping stove, a couple of beach chairs, and we were off.

Kate soon picked up a job in the local hospital. She was hired into the Behavioural Medicine Unit where she was assigned to eating disorders. Here she managed the food and medicine for female patients who were either bulimic, anorexic, or obese. These women also underwent extensive psychotherapy which invariably revealed that they had been sexually abused somewhere along the way, usually in childhood. But the strangest part of it was that after enough group therapy, which Kate routinely attended, their stories began to converge until they all had a similar tale.

Kate's limp still came and went though her stomach problems seemed to have gone away. And then one day she went blind for a few minutes. We had great health insurance, and the local Kaiser Permanente facility soon passed her from one specialist to another and then prescribed a new kind of test called MRI, magnetic resonance imaging, made possible in the last few years by rapidly advancing computer power. She asked me to come with her to get the results. The doctor showed us images that looked to me a lot like x-rays but she pointed out white spots on Kate's spine and in her brain.

"These are lesions," the doctor said, "on the nerve tissue. I have to say that these are consistent with Multiple Sclerosis."

Kate knew exactly what this meant and cried for days. It took me a while to catch up. This is a disease in which the body attacks the coating of the nerves running from the brain, down the spine to all parts of the body. It is unpredictable, affecting different people in different ways and progressing at different speeds. There was no known cause, no known prevention, and at that time no known treatment, and to this day no known cure. We had fought our way all the way to this paradise only to learn this.

We took the kids to Disneyland and waited in long lines for The Jungle Cruise, Pirates of The Caribbean, and Thunder Mountain. This was expensive and we wanted to make the most of it. We left the newest attraction, Star Tours, for last but there was still over an hour's wait. It was well past their bedtimes, but we each held one of them in our arms and woke them for the ride itself. We took them to every theme park and we went camping on every long weekend. The destinations were like the spokes of a wheel, some longer, some shorter. To the west we camped at every State

Beach Park from San Diego to Morro Bay. To the east we camped at nearby San Gorgonio National Forest and further east at San Jacinto above Palm Springs. We made it all the way to The Grand Canyon and Apache National Forest. To the north we could go as far as Sequoia National Forest and even Kings Canyon.

That first doctor with her MRI slides had correctly predicted that Kate had progressive MS. And despite her most courageous, stubborn resistance she now began an inexorable decline. For a while she got around with a walking stick but there came a point where we needed to rent a wheelchair to get around a theme park. And then there came the inevitability of a handicap placard for the vehicle, which was now a GMC Safari van. And finally, she acquiesced to a personalized wheelchair, a metallic purple one that she uses to this day. We added hand controls to the Safari van so she could continue to drive and that too lasted many years into the future.

Though Kate's prognosis cast a long shadow over our lives it is still hard to overstate the exhilaration we felt in this new life. California was America's America, the place the rest of the country looked to for inspiration, or came to for a better life. It was the zeitgeist of American society and the Western world at large. There were few innovations in any sphere that did not originate here, then spread across the country and then the whole world. As a society it was the leader in nutrition and exercise. The people were far healthier, far less obese, and far more environmentally conscious than anywhere else. California had pioneered unleaded gas, had banned offshore oil drilling, saved its sea otters and whales and condors and tortoises, and preserved millions of acres of its wildernesses far beyond the boundaries of its nine national parks.

The contrast to dear old Ireland was at times bewildering. At that time there was no immigration to Ireland, just centuries of emigration. We all looked and sounded the same. Here, people spoke dozens of languages and came from every corner of the world. The cities did not just have barrios and ghettoes and Chinatown and Little Italy, they had Vietnamese and Korean and Afghan enclaves. There were Buddhist monasteries and Hindu temples, Japanese nurseries, Chinese acupuncture salons, Vegan supermarkets, German beer gardens and Irish pubs, designed back home and shipped as kits to compete with the burgeoning microbrew industry. People bought luxury homes with gleaming fitted kitchens, then ate out all the time. Breast implants and nose jobs were commonplace. I read Robert Bly's *The Sibling Society* to make sense of it all. Guy Forney's wife took their dog to regular psychotherapy sessions.

There was more. I had climbed Ireland's three highest mountains, but even if you stacked them on top of each other they would not reach the nearby summits of San Gorgonio and San Jacinto. There were trees here as tall as our tallest buildings. There were temperature swings in a single day that exceeded the entire annual range back home. The weather itself was an entirely new experience. Back home the weather was unpredictable, and the forecast was always a subject of great interest after the nine o'clock news. It was usually bright spells with scattered showers, sometimes frost in the midlands, and maybe once a year a so-called heatwave, with temperatures soaring into the seventies Fahrenheit. Here they would announce on the news if there was weather coming. In other words most days there were sunny blue skies and you could fire up the grill. If a rainstorm was brewing over the Pacific you would get a weeks notice. if it was coming up from Hawaii carrying warm rain they called it a Pineapple Express.

Meanwhile, the westward migration of the rest of my family gathered pace. Mom and Dad bought a house in Simsbury, across town from the Nolans. It was a large, long bungalow, with a basement as was customary, but the previous owners had already fully converted this downstairs into bedrooms and a den. It had a large back lawn that gave way to the usual woods of birch and spruce that blanket all of New England. Anne came to live with them followed by Finbarr with his Civil Engineering degree in hand. Michael and Jackie made their way over and announced they were engaged. John Harney had been working his way up in the emerging financial software world in Dublin and nailed a position in New York City with his Irish employer, the inverse strategy of my own move.

In truth the rest of them were still closer to Dublin than to California but now we all began to plan trips back and forth. Mom and Dad were the first to visit. Although they had been to some business conferences here over the years, they really didn't know much about California. It put me in mind of one of his old oft-repeated supercilious parables about two Dublin factory girls who have just returned from a holiday in Italy but when he asks them whether they were on the Adriatic or Mediterranean coast they respond by saying: "I don't know, sure, we flew both ways." Bad-a-boom. Hilarious, at least to him. They were a bit past the theme park stage so we took them to see The Queen Mary and The Spruce Goose, which at that time was housed in a huge geodesic dome next to the ship, just across from Long Beach, a coast city embedded in the vast sprawl of Los Angeles County.

Dad was mesmerized by the sight of nodding donkeys, those reciprocating oil pumps that suck crude oil out of the ground and into a network of pipes that eventually take it to a refinery somewhere. It was mind-boggling to him that there was oil under the streets of a major city.

"So that's why there's so many Mercedes in California!"

And then the others arrived for their first-ever sun-soaked Christmas. I told Michael and Finbarr I would take them to March Air Force Base museum and the three of us piled into the Blazer and as I was backing out of the driveway Dad came bolting out the front door to join us. The irony was not lost on any of us. All those years he had kept us waiting on him, pent up in the car with Mom, while he dithered at God knows what, and now the tables were turned. We toured the flight line and marvelled at being in the presence of an actual Flying Fortress, then went indoors to look at exhibits of engines, propellors, and other flight paraphernalia. There was a full-size model of a Viet Cong guerrilla in a glass case. He wore black pajamas, flip-flops and a bamboo coolie hat. He was holding an AK-47 rifle and had a small bag of rice slung over his shoulder.

"These are the fellows who won. You know that don't you?" said Dad.

It was one of those many questions he was fond of asking where he implicitly knew something no one else did. It was not so much a rhetorical question as a challenge. Did you dare to disagree with his contrarian world-view on this or any other matter? All wider context was inadmissible. There was just this one bald statement of fact. Never mind that The Vietnam War, which had brought about upheaval in American society itself, and spawned the rock and roll generation of which I was a part, was just a battle in the decades-long Cold War, which was about to end with the pulling down of The Berlin Wall, the physical embodiment of Churchill's Iron Curtain. So who won?

We went to Sea World and San Diego Zoo and then it was our turn to fly back east for Michael and Jackie's wedding. They now lived in Dallas, but the wedding was held in a small church in Simsbury and the reception was hosted at Mom and Dad's. Finbarr had a new girlfriend, an Iraqi engineer from his work. Anne too was dating a guy named Kevin from The Cracker Barrel, the bar she worked at, where he was one of the chefs. John and Mary finally had some money in their pockets, Rex and Layla seemed little different to our own kids, and Mary had started going to college.

My own job was going well. The prospect of being moved to Iowa continued to haunt me but I came up with a solution. What if that factory ceased to exist? I put together an exercise using this new software program called a spreadsheet and presented my plan on mylar slides on an overhead projector showing that if we closed Ames, Iowa and moved all of its activities to Mexico, Puerto Rico, and Ireland we could save millions of dollars. The Iowa plant was duly wiped off the map and I was promoted to Director of Manufacturing Support, a similar job to Cork but with worldwide responsibility. We had now settled into Redlands, with Justin on the school swim team and, incredibly, we found an Irish dancing school and enrolled Helen in it, and through this met other Irish immigrants and became fast friends with a couple of families from Northern Ireland, musicians, who proudly displayed their Long Kesh awards in their living rooms. It was a standing joke that if you missed the Ould Sod just find a copy of The Irish Times, no matter the date, and the front page would have three headings: unemployment, emigration, and The North.

We now knew we lived in the world's fifth largest economy and increasingly accepted this was now our home. There were no jobs akin to what Kate was doing back in Ireland. And what would be the point of bringing Justin and Helen back there only to watch them leave again? California was the epicentre of high-tech, of entertainment, and even an agricultural powerhouse. Half of Silicon Valley was now foreign-born such was its allure. Millions of tourists flocked here every year to experience Disneyland and Universal Studios, microcosms of the escapism of the silver screen itself. Over half of all the fruit, vegetables and nuts consumed by the entire country came from our Central Valley. And now California had risen to be the world's fourth largest wine producer after Italy, France and Spain. And we grew every single varietal they all did and then some.

In the summer of nineteen-ninety the whole family converged on the small Maine seaside town of Bar Harbour. We had rented a large house on the beach that could hold all of us. As we left Bangor airport in our rental car we were amazed to see the first MacDonalds we passed advertising lobster sandwiches. We drove over the bridge that connects the mountainous island of Mount Deseret to the mainland and made our way to the house which was set in a deep inlet that cuts into the centre of the main island with lots of rocky outcrops and islets all around.

We were disappointed to find that there were no sandy beaches but we soon found a rushing stream that the kids could jump into from a rock, then float in their tubes underneath a tiny stone bridge, clamber out, and repeat. We found a place in town where you could pre-order cooked lobsters and gorged on this cheap-as-burger delicacy. Jackie booked us all on a whale-watching excursion, which took up a whole day and made the kids seasick, but we saw lots of humpbacked whales, or at least their huge flukes rising and falling.

Dad was tolerable when we played board games but he offered up very little about what was going on at work. Finbarr found a trail map of Acadia National Park and next day we set out on a long hike. Kate, Jackie, and Mom stayed at the house, but Dad started out with us. He soon became testy and then declared: "Ah, sure don't let me hold you all up!" We offered to go slower, or let him take the lead but he just sat down and then lay down on a rock.

It was as well he had not persisted because we soon found ourselves clinging to steel bars that had been pounded into the granite long ago to make it possible to navigate around narrow treacherous ledges with no other means of clinging to the smooth, slippery rock. We reached a wide spot and stopped to look down. Dad was still lying on the same rock.

"What is he like?" asked John. It was a rhetorical question because we all knew what an antichrist he could be at a moment's notice. But he had had his day. The patriarch's rule was over and we had all gone our own ways.

On the way back west Kate and the kids and I took a detour to New York City to see her sister, who was now living in The Bronx. For some reason we had a long wait at a train station where Kate checked to be sure Justin and Helen were buried in their Game Boys. Even still she led me out of earshot.

"I had a long talk with Mary," Kate began. quietly. "She's been going to therapy for a while now and she's finding out a lot about herself."

I could tell she was leading up to something.

"Have you ever heard of repressed memory syndrome?" she asked.

I shook my head.

"It's actually fairly common. When people are badly abused they bury the memory of what happened because it's the only way they can function normally."

I felt a sense of dread, not so much from Kate's words but because I could tell now she had been rehearsing this, waiting for an opportunity.

"You can recover those memories under hypnosis. Mary has done that. She says she knows now that your father sexually abused her. She's afraid to confront him with it but her therapist is helping her write a letter to him. She said not to tell you until after we left."

Chapter Ten. 1991 - 1992.

Gaze not too long into the abyss, lest the abyss gaze also unto thee.

Friedrich Nietzsche

At first I just could not wrap my head around this. If it wasn't true it was a monstrous allegation but if it was true my father was a monster and I was the son of a pedophile. I went over and over it every night with Kate. How old was Mary? She didn't know. Where did this happen? Again no answer. But Kate had been around many, many abused women and there were some tell-tale signs about Mary. Her personal hygiene was very slapdash, she didn't wear make-up and had no interest in fashion. In other words, she had low self-esteem.

Everyone had gone their separate ways after Bar Harbor but a couple of weeks later the accusatory letter arrived from Mary in New York. Dad's response was to read it out to all of us, clearly flabbergasted. And the words that Mary and her therapist had crafted were unambiguous: I know now that you sexually abused me when I was a child. Dad was generally a suspicious, secretive person, so to instantly broadcast this was out of character unless he really was genuinely shocked. He had kept Ena a secret for who knows how many years and he had kept Nessa a secret possibly for years as well. And who knew how many geisha girls he had shagged during his month-long trip to Japan.

And yet, if this had in fact happened, it was an order of magnitude worse than all of that. They were consenting adults. What he had done to Mary was what they called statutory rape, in other words, whether or not she had resisted him he had raped her. And why had she not told Mom? Kate pointed out that even most grown women were too ashamed to reveal that they had been raped. Mary as a little girl had had bedwetting issues which had been put down to weak kidneys.

What did Mom know about all of this? She too was a keeper of secrets. She would have taken what happened between Dad and Ena to her grave if she had not been so upset that night in The Phoenix Park and blurted it out. What other secrets were there? I just could not make sense of all this. And I had just been promoted again at work. I was now Vice-President

76

of Engineering, tasked with coming up with new products to win back our market share from the Japanese who had a huge lead in these new miniaturized surface mount devices.

As I often did when I was stressed out at work I set out early on a Saturday morning to hike to the top of San Gorgonio, a strenuous ten hour round-trip with a vertical mile of elevation gain, and just think about it all. The ascent began at Forest Falls, a popular picnic spot and waterfall a few miles from our house. The first couple of miles is a series of steep switchbacks through yucca and creosote but then it levels out to a rambling trail through the forest itself. I could now tell the ponderosas from the sugar pines and lodgepole pines. This too had been a marvel when I first explored it. Nothing like it existed in Ireland, nor for that matter on the East Coast. The trees were enormous, only outdone by the redwoods further north. Here and there the trail would cross a meadow to yet more trees. Blue jays abounded, mule deer occasionally scampered across the trail, and sometimes you heard a woodpecker.

This solitude was the tonic I needed. On other occasions I would replay important meetings but today I wanted to once and for all settle my thoughts about Mary and Dad. Was his hysterical reaction sincere or doth he protest too much? And then there was the matter of Mary's almost forgotten, or at least never mentioned, suicide attempt all those years ago. Not only was this act consistent with someone who had been abused, but Dad had blocked Mom's pleas for her to see a psychiatrist. Did he do that because he was afraid of what would come tumbling out as now seemed to be the case? The rest of the family seemed ambivalent, except for Mom, who plainly stated that she did not believe for a moment that Dad would be capable of such a thing.

My mind wandered over other strange memories. One night when I was twelve Dad came into the bedroom and felt my testicles when he thought I was asleep. So far as I knew, he only did it once, and I put it down to him checking that I was achieving puberty. There was all the yelling and tantrums that littered my otherwise pleasant childhood, being called a moron and an imbecile and an eejit and a gobshite. But was it right to condemn him for this latest unimaginable evil just because of his uncontrollable temper?

Where did the truth lie? When I was six years old we were still living in Clondalkin and I attended the same convent school and was taught by the same nuns as my father. Not just the same order of nuns but the very same nuns. However, this particular year our class, of about forty boys, had a substitute lay teacher, a Miss Clabby, who had long red hair and was much nicer and much younger than any of the nuns. She was always being called away on some business or other and would leave us with a dire warning that there was to be no talking until she returned. Her order would last all of a minute before some furtive whispering would start and then rapidly rise to a cacophony followed by games of chasing and horseplay until some lookout warned us all that Miss Clabby was in the corridor and we all dashed back to our seats such that when she re-entered the room she was greeted by forty silent motionless pupils.

"Stand up any boy who was talking while I was out of the room!" she demanded this particular morning.

The classroom was in fact the front half of the school's concert hall, pressed into service due to overcrowding, and her desk was up on the stage at the front. For whatever reason I was seated in the front row staring directly up at her. We all knew she had heard the racket which had only ended seconds before her return. I stood up.

"Who else was talking?" asked Miss Clabby, now standing behind her desk up on the stage.

I looked around to find that I was the only boy who had stood up.

"Come up here Seán Kenny," she ordered me and as I slowly climbed the steps at the side of the stage she picked up a wooden ruler from her desk. When I reached her she had me hold out my right hand and hit me on my palm three times and then the same on the left hand. I turned to leave shaking my tingling hands.

"Just a minute," said Miss Clabby. She reached into her bag and took out a banana. "Here, this is a reward for telling the truth."

I carried the precious fruit back to my desk and devoured it that lunchtime but the lesson lingered on all those intervening years and who's to say if that incident defined my relationship with the truth or what part it played in priming me for the unbearable dilemma I now faced.

The day warmed up and I peeled off my sweater, shoved it into my backpack, drank some water, and lathered on more sunscreen. I was walking along a ridge past stands of manzanita with its smooth red bark when I came across a juniper tree laden with its blue berries. I don't know why but it put me in mind of MotherKenny still living in the same house ever since we were born where she had long since planted an apple orchard and had a couple of gooseberry bushes and was immensely proud of all the different shrubs and trees she had grown over the years. I was in her kitchen and she was making blackberry jam, maybe that was the synapse.

Her favourite topic was running her children's spouses into the ground. The thought of Hilary's husband, Liam, would make her burst into tears chanting, "love is blind" over and over. She had a litany of insults for Uncle Michael's English wife and slightly less vicious mutterings for Ernie's and Tony's wives, but she never had a bad word to say about Mom. Auntie Nell, her sister, would invariably pop in the back door, as she lived in a cottage just walking distance away up the quarry lane, and the two of them were inseparable drinking partners. Their banter came back to me, most of it an inane take on the day's news, or endless repetition of family gossip. And then one phrase kept repeating in my head:

"That fella is as odd as two left feet."

It was MotherKenny and she was, of course, referring to her oldest son, Johnny, my father. She didn't denigrate her other four children, only him. We all knew by now that she had gotten pregnant with him before she was married. In fact she kept her age a closely guarded secret so we would not know just how young she had been when that happened. These exchanges routinely took place late at night after much alcohol had been consumed. This would also reliably cause Auntie Nell to break out into a few bars of *Under The Bridges Of Paris With You* or *How Much Is That Doggie In The Window* while she shadow waltzed herself around the kitchen. But when MotherKenny got to those words about Dad, sobbing into her ashtray, Auntie Nell would shout out:

"Oh, sure, they're all out of step except our Johnny!"

It was a riff on another old tune from her youth in which a mother is convinced all the soldiers are out of step except her son. But for these two uneducated, inarticulate old women these were their only words to express their psychological opinion. A simile about disfigurement and a line from an old soldier song. And yet there it was, he was not normal, even his own mother said so. He was non-conforming. There were huge gaps in his life interests. He had zero appreciation for the great food Mom endlessly provided him, just ate without comment. He had no interest in sports of any kind. He once took us to a Gaelic football game and once took us to motor racing in The Phoenix Park. He never took us to the movies, or went himself, nor did he go to the theatre, or even come to the Christmas pantomime if he could avoid it.

If you eschew all of this then what thoughts do fill up your head? Clearly extramarital sex was one of them. He had no real boundaries and his world view seemed to consist of a grab bag of prejudices and a belief that the whole world was against him. Mom would often say that he was his own worst enemy. I reached the juniper tree at the upper edge if the tree line and the trail petered out. You were left to make your own across the rocky peaks to the cairn that marked the summit. When I finally reached it I sat down to eat my sandwich at the top of the world.

Raping someone was bad enough, but this was apparently the violent rape of a child. And it was even worse than that. It was father-daughter incest, the worst of all possible betrayals. But now I had advanced my thinking from inconceivable, to conceivable, to believable. Too much of it lined up with other events. And there would only ever be circumstantial evidence. And here it was again, as the oldest child in a family that had an emotionally absent and at times highly abusive father, it fell to me to adopt that fatherly role.

I could not now abandon Mary to her fate, and if I did not stand up for her, no one would. I hated to believe her but what would happen if I told everyone I didn't? Would she go into a downward self-destructive spiral? And there were Rex and Layla to think about too. Her own mother did not believe her, could not believe her, could not now or ever accept that she had allowed this to happen to her daughter. I had thought all those years earlier on that beach in Spain that she was in tears at the thought of her only sister's imminent death but I knew now that there was far more going on and she needed me back in the family household because she could not turn to her treacherous husband for solace.

So there it was, once again, I would have to be the bigger man as Mom used to always tell me, and shoulder the fact that I was the son of a pedophile. I finished my lunch and kept just enough water to see me as far as High

Creek. The sweat on the back of my shirt had dried out now, so I slung on my backpack and began the long knee-buckling descent. No fresh thoughts on the matter came to me, I just sank into an almost unbearable depression, and that night when I went over it all with Kate and brought it all back to the surface, I was so nauseated I vomited over and over until I was left just throwing up my own green bile.

Kate did her best to assure me that I was not my father and that I was a good father and that my two children loved me, all of which was true but it did nothing to assuage these feelings. I took to going to bars on my own on the way home from work, self-medicating in the worst way. I felt distracted at work and knew even before I was told that my performance was becoming erratic. I searched around for self-help books on incest and soon came across *The Courage To Heal* by Ellen Bass and Laura Davis. You could hardly miss it as it was a huge bestseller and was usually displayed in bookstore windows. I called Mary to tell her about it, but she already had it, plus the accompanying workbook.

I had a PC set up in the spare bedroom which I mostly used to play Sim City and F14 Tomcat but now I loaded it with Microsoft Word and imported my eight chapters of novel that had gone untouched for the last seven years. More than ever I felt the need to reinvent myself, to not be in any way like my father, not be an engineer and a businessman, to be my creative self. I couldn't work on it in Kinsale because I did not have a PC. Having relocated to California I had been too busy with my job, exploring the American West, and raising Justin and Helen to work on it.

After a few months and no progress I realized that this was not just about the time sitting at the keyboard, it was about the enormous creative effort itself that is just impossible in the midst of constant pressure from all directions. Kate had quit her job some months earlier because her mobility was now just too compromised. She could still get around but being a nurse on a busy ward was too much. We had a low mortgage and we had some savings but we would have to have some income to stay afloat. And then, out of the blue, someone told Kate about a new kind of nursing job: home triage.

This was the age of the pager. How this worked was that Kate was employed by a PPO - a preferred provider organization - and incoming calls from their patients were routed to her pager. She then called the patients back and performed telephone triage. Based on what they then told her she instructed them, perhaps to just make an appointment with the doctor, or to go to an emergency room, or to call 911 immediately. This was an off-hours service so she mostly worked nights. We set up an office for her in our bedroom.

Back in the company we were in the throes of yet another reorganization and I was one of the managers deciding who would stay and who would go. It was now or never. I walked into Forney's office and told him I was burned out and asked if I could go on the layoff list. Under questioning I told everyone I was going to write a novel. Back in Ireland everyone I knew thought I was stark raving mad when I first started down that path, but here everyone was supportive, wished me luck, told me anecdotes about other writers, and were genuinely curious about the whole thing.

Having been laid off I could now claim unemployment, which would buy us even more time. I moved the PC out onto the upstairs landing which was shadier and cooler than the bedroom, bought myself a typist's chair and tried my best to put aside all thoughts of child molestation. This was it, my one shot at writing the great Irish novel.

Chapter Eleven. 1992.

Then God said, "Let there be light," and there was light.

Genesis 1:3-25

I set myself a quota of twelve hundred words a day. Some days I made this handily while others seemed to crawl excruciatingly along. But at this pace you can write the first draft of a novel in a few weeks. I devoured how-to-do-it books. I joined a writers group at the local bookstore, yes, in those days every town in America had at least one independent bookstore. I took a writing course at the local community centre. The lady who taught it would read writing samples but she was more focused on the correct use of "its" and "it's" than whether the work was really speaking to the human condition.

I subscribed to Writer's Digest and bought their all-important guide to publishers, agents, and editors. I went to a writers conference in San Diego where you could pitch story ideas and attend panels of agents and editors touting themselves and discussing trends. There were even sessions on screenwriting with Hollywood agents. It was all very exciting and I could now put a face to a few of the hundreds of names in my guidebook. At the same time, the prospect of breaking into the US publishing world remained very, very daunting.

There was an etiquette to all of this. Some agents wanted an outline and three chapters, most only read certain genres, many stated that they would not consider your work if you were doing multiple submissions, sending the same material to other agents. It was unclear how they would know this, but in any event this all cost money since every submission was a bulky packet with a large self-addressed stamped envelope for their response.

And soon the rejections started to flow in. Generally, these were just hand-written scribbles on my own cover letter wishing me all the best. There were also agents who you could pay to read your work, but after a couple of tries at this I realized this was just a mug's game since none of the feedback was of any real use. And yet by far the most difficult part of the whole enterprise was to keep going in the absence of any approval or encouragement by anyone who might know more about this than I did myself.

After about four months, I completed the first draft of The Ulstermen. I knew this was far too long for a first novel, but felt you could sell it as two trade paperbacks, parts one and two. Anyway it was done now. I added a map, a glossary of Irish words and a pronunciation guide and put it aside. Lots of writers advised this, pound out a first draft while keeping your inner editor in check, take a good break, then come back and edit it since otherwise there was the danger that you would never finish.

We packed up our camping gear and took off north toward Las Vegas, a four hour drive if the traffic was light. We stayed the first night at Circus Circus, the kids now tall enough to get on most of the rides. Next day we set out again early and reached Arches National Park in the afternoon. There was no need to pitch our tent since there wasn't a cloud in the sky. Justin was happy to sleep on the roof and we could rotate the two front seats to create a couple of beds for Kate and I. Helen snuggled up in her sleeping bag in the back. Next day we hiked around for a bit but I felt bad leaving Kate alone in the van reading her book, so we packed up and drove south to Moab where you could book rafting trips on the Colorado River. Mostly we just floated along but there were occasional rapids that thrilled the kids.

We stayed in a motel in Moab that night. I visited the bookstore where they proudly displayed a first edition of Edward Abbey's Desert Solitaire. The owner was a cantankerous fellow, who, when I asked him if they had any books on what had happened to the Anasazi, just told me no one knew, but they probably just hunted the local deer out of existence and starved to death. Next morning we drove south all day to Flagstaff, stopping at Canyon De Chelly to see the Anasazi cliff dwellings and then at Petrified Forest to see the eponymous trees. We took a detour to Sedona where I bought a Kachina doll, carved from a single piece of cottonwood by a Hopi artist, then drove to Needles, on the Colorado, to another motel, and then completed our loop westward through Palm Springs and back home.

There were of course no cell phones in those days but we returned to find the light flashing on our wall phone in the kitchen, which had a built-in answering machine. It was a message from Mom saying to call her.

"I just had another awful row with your father," she began, "and you know he's drinking a half bottle of whiskey a day. He keeps telling me that what he did with Ena wasn't wrong, that it was common practice in Ireland to have more than one wife until the Catholic church put a stop to it."

I could tell she was tearing up. "I don't believe what Mary is saying about him. I think she believes it but I just don't think it happened. Under all our noses? I know, I know, I didn't find out about Ena for years. But when I went to the altar with your father I had no intention of sharing him with another woman, and he knew that..."

"Of course he did," I told her.

"I don't know what to do Sean."

She was inconsolable. Dad had quit his job with Bob Nolan and had now started a software business that had something to do with data mining. And Michael had started investing his money in this venture which was yet another cause of consternation. And Jackie was pregnant. Mom herself was now working as an accountant at a small local manufacturer.

"Mom, I think you should just leave him." It was the only thing I could think of to say to her. What was the point in staying? Would some vengeful god really send her to hell for not suffering more and more pain from this man? She had raised her family and gone back into the workplace. Why endure any more of this? He was not going to change.

I plunged back into my writing world. I decided to just work on another entirely different first draft and began writing about the business world which led me to embezzlement and sexual harassment but eventually it took on the same shape as *The Ulstermen*. The overriding theme of my own existence was betrayal. It kept bubbling up over and over again. I even tried to write a science fiction novel about a future war between a Gaiaist peace-loving earth and a colonized militant Mars. Again it became a version of *The Ulstermen,* but I did send out some chapters of this and got some positive feedback of the "needs work" variety. I was in a rut and I desperately needed to find some new direction.

We had acquired a small dog for the kids, who named him Max, after Maxwell Smart, the secret agent on the Nickelodeon channel. He was a Pomeranian mix, fiercely loyal to all of us, but hated other dogs, of every size, which was what had landed him in the pound. Justin now also had a pet black King Snake who, to Helen's horror, we fed live mice. He was a clever snake, who learned to push the lid of his terrarium aside if we forgot to put the pin back after feeding him. He liked to hide in the springs of the couch but we always found him and as long as your hands were clean he didn't bite. And there it was, a story about animals. Some were fierce and some gentle, but you knew what you were getting. There might be conflict but the very notion of betrayal, of good and evil of any kind, just did not exist in the animal kingdom.

I already had an idea for this story. Kate had bought me *To The Waters And The Wild*, a memoir by the naturalist Gerrit Van Gelderen, about his wildlife film-making in Ireland. One photo in particular held my attention - a telephoto shot of a blue-winged teal on a sandy shore in Dublin. These birds only occur in The New World and this was a rare instance of one blown off course all the way across the Atlantic. I wrote a story about an out of step duck. All of the characters in the story are birds with personalities that reflect their species. Some help and some hinder this lone visitor in his search for his own kind. I wrote it in the first person to allow the blue-winged teal to express his feelings of loss at being separated from his family and flock. I sent the manuscript to three Irish publishers and then returned to revising *The Ulstermen*.

We received another disturbing phone call from my parents. Finbarr had been drinking at The Cracker Barrel the previous night and on the way home driving Mom's car he had skidded on a patch of ice, ran into a tree, and the car caught fire with him trapped in it. He had been taken by helicopter to a burn unit in Boston and they were treating him as we spoke. He would live but he would be permanently scarred. Over the next few months, at Dad's urging, Finbarr found an ambulance chasing law firm and sued Ford. They settled and Finbarr moved to Hawaii to take up surfing and try to find a job before the money ran out.

Soon after this Mom called to say she had had enough of Dad and that she was moving into an apartment they owned in Hartford. She came over on her own that Christmas and when I met her at the airport I was surprised at how small she now seemed. She drank a lot of wine and Kate and I noticed how little interest she took in the two grandkids. We took her to see *Les Miserables* in Los Angeles which we knew would be the high point of her trip. Mistakenly, I probed her one night about whether everyone else's family was just like this, which brought on tears as she reminisced about her father saying on his deathbed that neither of his daughters were ever a spot of bother to him and that she had never heard raised voices and shouting growing up until she met the Kennys.

Kate's multiple sclerosis now consumed her. Sometimes I had to carry her upstairs to bed. We joined the local MS Society chapter and supported fundraising walks. She was accepted into an interferon trial, but this new drug brought no improvement. She began to hear about all kinds of strange remedies, like bee stings, and drinking Coca-Cola all day. But then she read about a man in LA who had cured himself through yoga and promptly joined a local yoga class. Her instructor was a well-to-do divorcée who took a great interest in Kate and one day she came to the house, helped Kate into her red Porsche Boxster and they sped off to LA to meet this guru and attend one of his classes.

This set off an entirely new chain of events. Another Irish woman at that class, also an MS sufferer, detected Kate's accent and struck up a conversation with her. She, it turned out, was the wife of Fred Haines, who wrote the screenplay for the ninetee sixty-seven adaptation of James Joyce's Ulysses. In that movie the role of Gerty MacDowell, a Dubin prostitute, was played by Fionnula Flanagan, who had since moved to Beverly Hills where she was now married to prominent psychiatrist Garret O'Connor, a fellow Dubliner. Kate returned with a flyer about a weekend workshop on the subject of trans-generational shame which Doctor O'Connor was about to put on. It was called *Return To Innocence*.

Since this was an overnight event in West Hollywood we had no choice but to bring the kids but they were now old enough to amuse themselves in the back of the room. This was the single most eye-opening event I had ever attended. Garret O'Connor did most of the two days of talking, interspersed with some guided meditation with all of us lying on the floor while he had us imagine ourselves choosing a particular door. One of these was so upsetting to Kate it caused her to burst into tears because it released some pent-up feelings from her own much-troubled childhood. But the meat of this was his skillful combination of laying out the causes of the Irish shame-based society, which he richly illustrated with his own personal experiences.

There was a pattern, going back centuries, of the subjugation of the Irish Catholic majority by an Anglo-Irish Protestant minority. And it had taken a terrible toll and given rise to a society whose main outlet for dealing with being made to feel inferior to the conquering race and ashamed of themselves was to consume alcohol of all kinds, the cheaper the better, what Doctor O'Connor referred to as psychic numbing juice. And this came down through the generations as our shame-based parents passed on their shame to us, and on and on. It was a brilliant explanation for why the Irish were the way they were. It did not just apply to Irish Catholics. The entire indigenous population of North America who had been herded into barren reservations had similar problems as did African Americans, still dealing with the legacy of slavery. And the post-colonial societies of Africa and Australasia had this in spades too.

He carefully explained the difference between guilt and shame. We feel guilty for something we have done that we know was not right. But we can make amends for our actions. We can apologize, we can go to confession, we can do jail-time, and once we do we can go on to live better lives. We can simply choose not to do those things again. But shame is altogether different, it is not something we do, it is something we are. He also coined the term 'malignant shame', which I had never heard of before. There was narcissism, which could be just annoying, and there was malignant narcissism, with its remorselessness, which gave rise to all kinds of criminals and tyrants. Malignant shame, it seemed to me, robbed us of our ability to feel good about ourselves, and if we succumbed to it we passed it on to those around us. It was one thing to do one or two shameful things, feel some remorse and move on, but how can you do that if you are simply ashamed of who you are?

Language is consciousness. We must name our fears, we must identify our demons, if we are to confront them. And now for the first time I had been handed a rational explanation for so much of the turmoil I felt all my life. Although my education was highly technical, I had a huge interest in Irish history. I read the various tomes by Lee, Foster, Kiberd and *The Great Hunger* (eventually) and *The Great O'Neill* and *Rebels* and saw the plays of O'Casey and Friel and grew up touring castles and forts and abbeys and stone circles. But now, at last, I had a glimpse of the psychology of the whole thing. I was lit up just as that shaft of light penetrates through total darkness to the central chamber of Newgrange at dawn on the winter solstice. I now began to see the roots of the sadism of the Irish Catholic Church. And the reasons for the masochism of the rest of the population that had been so long in thrall to these clerics began to dawn on me. This was brilliant stuff and I came away from it all bristling with ideas for another book.

Chapter Twelve. 1993 - 1994.

Through The looking Glass
Lewis Carroll

The days and months flew by. The rejection letters kept coming but I had by now sent both my children's novel and what turned out to be an inches-thick tome of *The Ulstermen*, when printed out double-spaced, to Wolfhound Press in Dublin at their request. I had gone back to work at my old company as a consultant to manage the shutdown of a factory in Ogden, Utah, a six-month assignment that refilled our bank account. Now I was back at the keyboard working on my new novel exploring the trans-generational origins of why Irish society in general was such a terrible web of secrets and lies.

If any further proof was needed about Dad, Mary now provided it in spades. She had been an on-again off-again career student since coming to America but now she was well on her way to completing her degree in Women's Studies, consistently making the Dean's list. And she was diligently planning to spend an entire summer on a road trip across America with Rex and Layla. They would come west via a southerly route, ending up at our house from Arizona, which they did. John, who only had a limited amount of vacation time, flew over to join up with us.

Mary showed us a scrapbook of all the places they had been on the trip over. She had made notes and pasted in postcards and memorabilia and a foldout map of the USA with their route highlighted on it. She had no interest in taking her kids to expensive theme parks but both families were well equipped with camping gear and we now planned the next leg of her trip which would take us to a destination that had eluded the California Kennys up till now, being just too far for a long weekend, but that was very much still on our must-see list - Yosemite National park.

We set out early, taking the freeway north over the Cajon Pass, then west toward Palmdale, with the Mojave desert on our right and the San Gabriel mountains on our left, veering north again for a couple of hours, until the turnoff for the Tehachapi pass that would lead us down into the San Joaquin valley on the west side of the Sierras. I pointed out the long, long trains to the kids and explained that all rail traffic had to come through this pass and pulled over to show them the Tehachapi Loop where the front of the train literally passes over the trailing cars in its ascent to the summit.

We reached the south entrance to Yosemite late in the afternoon and drove along the meandering mountain road through pristine pine forests until suddenly the valley opens up in front of you with its spectacular granite walls and you descend along a road that has been blasted into the near-vertical face of one side of this glacier-gouged canyon. We crossed over the Merced River on a bridge of hewn granite blocks and made our way up a side canyon to our camp sites in the forest. Tents pitched, John and I set about starting a campfire, then broke out graham crackers, marshmallows and skewers for the kids and passed around bottles of cold American beer to each other.

The following morning we all drove down to Yosemite Village to meet Finbarr off the bus. It was the first time I had seen him since his accident. He had noticeable scarring and skin grafts on his left arm but other than that he looked great. He was lean and suntanned and just as excited as all of us to be here. Like me, Finbarr had thoroughly researched Yosemite and by the time we had all finished our cafeteria lunch we had a good idea of what we wanted to do over the coming days. There were the waterfalls, of course, and there was hiking, and redwood trees. We spent that afternoon touring around the valley floor, taking the kids on short hikes into the bases of waterfalls. They swam in the pools, jumped off rocks, wore themselves out and crashed early, leaving the five of us to sit around the campfire and talk.

None of us had been to Hawaii other than Finbarr so he regaled us with stories of surfing and scuba-diving and bull sharks and turtles. But the main topic was Mom's decision to move back in with Dad. I learned that she had in fact called all five of us and not just me to assure her we would not cut off contact with her if she did this. He had been relentless in pursuing her, endlessly promising her he would change and be better and kinder to her. One of her co-workers had taken a romantic interest in her and it seems we had all encouraged her to go that direction, but in the end she had decided that her marriage vows were sacred and she would not break them. She was just desperately lonely, so she would give him a second try.

We did not talk about Mary and Dad. Mary was clearly in a much better place now and if she didn't bring it up we did not feel we should. It was still an almost incomprehensibly vile thing to have happened, but we now knew this was much more common than we thought, affecting one in three girls according to Courage To Heal. I thought it was probably even higher than that in Ireland with its overarching culture of lies and hypocrisy and its celibate clerics of every ilk around every corner. The Irish had learned over the generations to hide everything lest it be taken from them or used against them.

The next day Finbarr, John, and I set out early to hike Half-Dome, while the others slept in and would later drive over to Mariposa Grove to tour the giant Sequoias. This was a brutal hike in three segments - stone step switchbacks up the side of Vernal Falls, then a long break across a meadow to the base of the dome, and then a climb to the top using steel cables set into the rock to pull yourself along. And yes, half of this granite dome is missing, and you could peer over the vertical face and see climbers below making their way up the face of it. The descent was equally gruelling, and we wobbled painfully to the shuttle bus back to The Ahwahnee Hotel to meet up with everyone else.

The following morning Kate ferried Finbarr, John, me and the four kids up to Glacier Point. From here we would hike back down to the valley floor. This was an easy well maintained switchback trail and at various points we stopped to identify the various landmarks that came into view. At one of these pauses I happened to look over and see Rex picking up a rock and dropping it off the edge.

"Rex! Don't do that! There are people on the trail below us. You could hit someone," I yelled.

Rex grinned sheepishly back at me. I shook my head and we walked on, and then, incredulously, he did it again. He picked up another rock and heaved it over the edge.

"What is wrong with you?" I shouted. "I told you there are people down there and you could hurt someone!"

This time there was no grin, just a defiant stare. John also chimed in and told him to stop but after this I just watched him like a hawk all the way down and he watched me back, apparently hoping I would get distracted and give him yet another opportunity to smash in the brains of some unfortunate tourist. Justin was a difficult defiant child and it was not until Helen following along two years behind him in elementary school started to bring home citizen of the month awards with their Uncle Howie's pizza coupons that we knew such things existed. Helen was the darling of all the mothers on our street, Justin was always climbing some tree he shouldn't.

When Justin was very young he would crawl around the floor of the local supermarket turning off the freezers but as he grew older we held him more accountable. When he was doing something he shouldn't I would tell him to stop, then if he persisted I would threaten him with the wooden spoon, and if that didn't work I would actually give him a couple of slaps on the hand with it, which I hated doing, but it did seem to work. And Rex was now eleven years old and had clearly understood what I said. He just chose consciously to ignore me and do what he wanted to do anyway, knowing it was wrong and dangerous to other people. Something was missing here. It wasn't just as if the people further down the trail whose lives he was putting in danger did not exist, or if they did that they didn't matter, but it was as if he was able to erase my words because they did not align with what he wanted to do, as if he could negate my existence.

John worked full time and Mary stayed at home which had been the arrangement ever since Rex had been born. Ours was different, both because I needed to help a lot more with the cooking and shopping and because in these last few years I had really been Mister Mom, walking the kids to school, then being there when they got home when Kate might still be asleep before her night shift. Did Mary not observe similar bad behaviour by Rex? Or was he careful and cunning enough to conceal it from her? Had Rex just miscalculated what he could get away with here? To be sure, Mary lectured her children about their behaviour, but I never saw any real consequences.

We spent the last night at the campsite chatting about this and that. Dad did not come up at all. I wondered about Finbarr and his decision to exile himself to Hawaii. He knew nobody there so it must be a lonely existence and there was certainly nothing stopping him from returning at any point.

He was a gentle, inoffensive person, invisible a lot of the time in our family, therefore avoiding the mayhem at holiday times. But how had Mary's letter affected him? Or Mom and Dad splitting up? In the wake of his accident he had clearly come to a decision that the whole thing was too painful to be around. He was never as wild as the rest of us, in fact was the most bookish of us all, so I had to wonder if this horrific incest revelation was the root cause of his reckless drinking and driving and if that was what had led to this near-death experience and his decision to flee halfway around the world.

We went our separate ways the next day. Finbarr and John flew west and east respectively from San Francisco, Mary and her kids drove north to continue their long loop across the country, and we retraced our way south. Back home our kids whiled away the summer at the pool or on the trampoline that Santa had brought the previous Christmas. All nine of the houses on our street shared a common set of mailboxes mounted on a steel column which I could see from our living room. I became obsessed with it, like some strange sundial, and tried to calculate by observing the angle of the shadow of the steel support column whether the post had arrived and I should walk across the street and see who had rejected me now.

And then one day later that year, with a Santa Ana wind whipping the tree branches around, I found a letter with an Irish stamp on it and hurried back across the street to open it. It was from Wolfhound Press in Dublin, and it contained a cover letter and a three-page contract. They were going to publish my children's book, giving it the title *Fast-Wing* after the duck who narrates the tale. There was a minuscule advance, but after all this time it was validation enough. I had written a story that an actual bona fide publisher was confident they could turn into a book that people would pay money for in bookshops. I would soon be a published author of a book-length work of fiction. It had happened.

Christmas came and went and then it was nineteen ninety-four. By now I had finished my story about trans-generational shame. This was also set entirely in Ireland, so although I had sent it to a few New York agents, who found the protagonist so unlikeable they did not want to read on, I began to strategize on how to pitch this to Wolfhound Press or any other Irish publisher. Wolfhound had accepted one manuscript, were still sitting on the much larger one, and had, as I knew from scouring titles in Irish book shops, published novels not unlike either *The Ulstermen* or this new one to which I had given the working title *Cannibal Society*.

There were no issues with the length of this new novel. It was a very dark story but it followed all the rules. Should I just print out the manuscript and lob it over the pond to them? Or would that just piss them off? Would they take that as a lack of appreciation for the risk they were taking on this first kid's book? After all, they now had to hire an editor, an illustrator, a publicist, and print an economic quantity of books, distribute them and hope for the best. Understandably they might want to see how all that turned out before investing more time and money in my direction.

Life at home was not going so well at this point. Kate valiantly resisted allowing her MS to get in the way of a normal life. But the downside of this was that we all had to go at her pace. She complained that she found it hard to work on the phone with my snoring. And we seldom shared the same bed at the same time anymore. I was rattled by the fact that I had now taken over all parenting duties - school, sports, Irish dancing, swimming, and now Justin's guitar lessons. He was obsessed with Kurt Cobain and Nirvana's songs. Kate and I seldom left the house other than when I had to buy groceries or use a two-for-one coupon at Little Caesar's Pizza.

We were like the proverbial frog in the pot. It wasn't boiling yet, but it was starting to simmer. And maybe that's what finally solidified a plan in my mind. I would go to Ireland and camp out with friends until I could get a meeting with Wolfhound Press. I now at least knew the name of the publisher there, Seamus Cashman. I sent back the contract with a short letter saying I was planning a trip and would call to set up an appointment to meet him while I was there. I still found the whole world of writing and publishing both mysterious and frightening and had no idea if this was pushing my luck or was some huge breach of etiquette that I might soon regret.

Chapter Thirteen. 1994.

There are two sides to every story.

My mother.

The horror of what my father had done gnawed away incessantly at me. I thought I might have purged some of it with my latest novel but I had not included any mention nor even a hint of incest in that story, hewing carefully to how Ireland's holocaust had given rise to generations of shame. I was of course ashamed myself to be the progeny of a pedophile monster but as of yet had no other strategy than that of proving to myself that I was not like my father by taking myself to a world he could never enter. Were he to live for a thousand years he would not compose a novel, nor take to any other form of art because he was simply artless.

I had never seen the letter Mary wrote and never would. I knew snippets of it from various conversations and I knew through Kate that her therapist had suggested it as a safe way to confront him. Even that need to accuse him from a hundred miles distance added to the malice of it all. He was a violent bad-tempered man and he would explode and it would be highly dangerous to be in the same room while revealing such a thing. I remained obsessed with it all and the aphorism that we write to right our lives kept coming back to me.

I kept seeing this letter, then seeing Mary writing it in her therapist's office, reading it back to him, or maybe it was a her, then folding it up, sliding it into the envelope, licking the envelope shut, writing Dad's name and address on it, licking the stamp, and then for some reason opening the metal flap on one of those waist-high square blue and red metal mailboxes with the bald eagle's head logo, then hesitating, and then finally deciding and dropping it inside. Did Mary consider or even imagine how that irreversible act would alter, not just her own life, but those of all of the rest of her family?

An idea began to take shape in my head. What if I simplified all of this to its essence, a daughter accusing her father of incest from far away? There was by no means enough material here for a full length novel, but there was for a short story. But the market for short stories was a thing of the past so what other vehicle might there be to get this story noticed? It was too short and too lacking in movement to be a candidate for a movie, or even a short film. What about a stage play?

Back in Dublin we had been regular theatre-goers, excited when the next Hugh Leonard or Brian Friel play was advertised in The Irish Times. The city had half a dozen venues, some big, some small. The more avant-garde plays would go to one of those, plays that had a small cast and simple set design. What if I made this a one man play that takes place in the front room of a typical small Dublin home, and we see the whole story unfolding as an embittered old man's routine is shattered by the arrival of this letter?

The play would be a monologue, but I had seen that work before. Sure, he would be talking to himself, but the soliloquy was an accepted device going back at least as far as Shakespeare's *Hamlet.* We, the audience willingly accept that the actor is speaking out loud merely as a device to reveal the thoughts of the character. If I placed the daughter on the other side of the pond the idea of a letter made even more sense plus it fed into the possibility that she had fled Ireland to escape her past. This medium was new to me but I knew someone who could help me with it.

It did not take very long to write this and doing so was truly cathartic. Everything the central character says is something I heard my father say. He is a grab bag of grievances and contradictions. He is the stereotypical Irish begrudger. All the world is against him but he knows everything and they know nothing. As I worked my way through this I did conclude I would at least have to include the voice of the daughter in it even if she never comes on stage. I revised it a couple of times and then sent it to Maureen Donegan in Rome.

The Donegans were old family friends going back to my early childhood. They didn't live close to us but they would visit whenever they were up in Dublin and we would occasionally but less frequently visit them in Cork. They had a daughter my age but she was drawn to older more sophisticated sailors than me at the yacht club dances and two sons a couple of years younger. Maureen Donegan was the only actual professional writer I had ever met. Her biggest area of success was radio drama. She sold several radio plays to the BBC and took over writing *The Riordans,* Ireland's longest running soap opera, set on a farm somewhere, when it was moved from television to radio. She wrote hundreds of episodes and would explain to us that the biggest challenge was that she had to give each of the major characters, Tom, Mary, Benjy, Batty Brennan and others a minimum number of lines every season per their contracts.

When her kids grew up Maureen parted ways with her husband and when her daughter married an Italian and moved to Italy she moved to Rome where she worked as a translator for the UN's FAO - Food and Agriculture Organization. She had come to see us once with my mother and they had done the usual - Hearst Castle, San Juan Capistrano and The Getty Museum - plus some trips around the desert with all of us. A frugal Yorkshire woman, she constantly chided me for over-tipping, saying you would never do that in Europe. But she was an enormously encouraging presence in my writing life, reading and commenting on the poems I wrote as a teenager and now I knew she would help guide me through this. I sent her the manuscript and she sent it back duly annotated and confirmed that it would need a second character, the daughter.

I revised it again and then took it to Fionnula Flanagan, who invited me to her home in Beverly Hills to discuss it. She knew about it, and knew about the abuse from one of the other writers who I had gotten to know at one of the *Return To Innocence* workshops. Fionnula was at this point possibly Ireland's most famous actress, beginning her career on stage in Dublin and going on to play the part of Gerty McDowell in the 1967 movie of James Joyce's *Ulysses,* followed by a slew of silver screen and TV roles .That afternoon we talked a bit more about moving the project forward and she suggested that the next step should be to do a reading of it. I drove home on cloud nine. (I have published it as an e-book on Amazon entitled *A Fitting End* for anyone who is curious.)

My elation at the approval of two women who I hugely admired soon gave way to yet more turmoil. Putting on a little stage play would not be very expensive so this was certainly a viable idea. There was little point launching it in Los Angeles where the significance would be lost on most people. Sure there were ten million people here but very few had any Irish connection and the intersection of those who did and those who actually ever went to see a stage play and just the sprawling footprint of this place and would more than a tiny handful brave the infamous traffic to come and see the thing?

The obvious solution to that would be to put it on in Dublin. In that case every single person in the audience would be from Dublin or its surrounding area. I doubted that it would cause a repeat of The Playboy Riots - *"not if all the girls in Mayo were lined up in front of me in their shifts would I choose one of them over you, Pegeen,"* - and the audience erupted in indignation at this affront to Irish womanhood, but that was nineteen-o-seven, not the last decade of the twentieth century. Nevertheless, Holy Catholic Ireland was still in the ascendant. Contraception remained heavily regulated, divorce was still three years in the future, and abortion would not be legalised for another quarter of a century.

Whatever the reaction of the public in general to a play set entirely in the mind of a pedophile schoolteacher there was the even more troubling and highly likely possibility that people would figure out who I was writing about - my own father. Not that I gave a tinker's dam about that, but by extension I would be broadcasting the fact that my mother had allowed this to take place. She would quite literally never be able to show her face in public, in Ireland, again. And it would be impossible to dodge the issue since any half decent journalist would ask and any reviewer would at least speculate on it.

Mary's letter had thrown our own family into chaos and this was just throwing fuel on the fire. What would it accomplish? Dad would just continue to deny that any of this had happened, and in fact, with the possible exception of Anne, so would the rest of the family. I had no idea if even Mary herself would welcome this. On top of that it was almost certain that even though people would figure out who I was writing about that still was absolutely no guarantee that anyone would believe it was true and would just see it as an incredibly lurid and distasteful publicity grab on my part. It might very well be panned for that reason, and without some good reviews it would be canceled within a week.

But was it right not to go ahead out of fear of the consequences? And if that really was what stayed my hand did that make me just a craven fraud? My novel about Irish shame was soon going to be published, was this not enough? But that tackled a broader social problem, the trans-generational shame of those who had not perished while millions of others had. This was different, it pointed the finger right into the living rooms and bedrooms of Ireland. It suggested that sexual abuse was commonplace, as indeed it was and still is. It is impossible to know the full extent of it since so much of it goes unreported, but from the time when Irish girls living in thatched cottages had their ankles tied together at night to the age of online porn, sexting and webcams, the proclivity of men with power to abuse powerless young girls, throw in the endless Catholic Church scandals and payoffs, and add young boys, is ever-present.

When Oedipus realized he had married his own mother he gouged his own eyes out. What if Mary was not telling the truth? I had never witnessed any of this, nor had anyone. My mother had the misfortune to stumble on her sister in flagranté with her husband but there was no such corroborating evidence here. This was all circumstantial. Did I have the right to subject my whole family to this inevitable opprobrium when I had no proof that any crime had occurred? Certainly it was my strong belief that Mary was abused given her self-destructive behaviour and subsequent turnaround and why would she accuse Dad if there was some other perpetrator? Why not just name that person?

This was a truly baffling predicament. My father was a terrible person but the sum of all his other known misdeeds was still not a justification for inflicting this on him. To simply say he almost certainly did it because he was a sadist with no moral bearings of any kind was not enough. This was truly to be or not to be, to bite the apple, to lick the salmon, or indeed as the Bard put it, thus conscience doth make cowards of us all, and there was no threading this bodkin, this was a do or die moment, though it may well have been the longest moment of my life. In the end it was not the subatomic particle of doubt that stayed my hand, but the love I felt for my mother who was the living proof of what awful things can befall those so utterly undeserving of such suffering and I could not go forward knowing this would surely be yet another burden for her to bear.

Chapter Fourteen. 1994 - 1995.

Give me chastity, Lord, but not yet.

Confessions
Saint Augustine

I flew to Ireland to see if I could if I could use force of will, or just grovel, to advance matters. This was still a time of phones that were attached to the wall and exorbitant long distance phone call costs. And since I intended to move around from place to place I had to leave messages and then call back again. Car rental was also beyond my reach, so, with the help of Kate's brother, Michael, who was a Garda sergeant in Dublin, I bought an old car for cash. He made a fake registration sticker for the windshield and I threw my suitcase in the back and hit the road.

I called Wolfhound Press and spoke to their receptionist. She said Mister Cashman was tied up but to call the following Monday by which time she would be able to talk to him about a meeting. I had a couple of friends with high-brow literary tastes, so I dropped off a copy of my new manuscript with Colman in Drogheda, then headed south to Cork to stay with Billy Corr, who I had known since we were teenagers, had been best man at my wedding, and was now back in Ireland after several years in the oil industry in Borneo and Holland. There was one other person who I really wanted to talk to and that was Steve, an American writer who was now married to Mary's just about oldest friend, Geraldine. I had known her since she was a child, because she was always coming and going, although I did not know that this was because her father was a raging alcoholic and when he was off the wagon my mother would help out her mother by taking in one of the two daughters. I had only met Steve once when they came by our home in Dublin before we had left for America, and I had not seen Geraldine either in the intervening years.

The trip to Cork was mostly uneventful and over Guinness and Hamlet cigars in the local pub I was lectured on not making any changes to my work, that art is art, take it or leave it and did I think Shakespeare or Joyce let others meddle with their words? I pointed out that even Hemingway took writing lessons which took the conversation to a whole new level of derision.

In Billy's view Hemingway was nothing but a hack and it was one of the great travesties of literary history that he had been awarded the Nobel prize, especially when Joyce had not. There would be no help from this quarter. I drove down to Kinsale for old time's sake to find that our house, and half the hillside behind it, had been demolished and replaced with a far larger luxury home, presumably at great cost, and smiled and shook my head at how privileged we had been to live in that postcard for those three years.

Then I drove to Galway. My uncle, Tony, had heard I was coming to Ireland and wanted me to visit. At this point he was separated from his wife and I met him at his then girlfriend's house where she made us dinner.

"Where is Mary getting this shite about Johnny molesting her" he asked as we finished our poached salmon. He was clearly very agitated about it all. Dad and Tony were close, even though Tony was at least ten years younger than him. They fought on and off, usually after a few drinks, but Tony was always there for him, whether it was politics, business, the much-hated Catholic church that had excommunicated their own father for taking up arms against the British, or the latest American atrocity in the Middle East, or now the break-up of the Balkans.

"I wish I didn't believe it," I began, "but if you look at the evidence it's hard not to."

"What evidence?" Tony demanded. "Nobody saw him do it!"

I took a deep breath. "Mary attempted suicide as a teenager, and then Dad blocked her from getting psychiatric help." Tony had a degree in psychology. "And she was a screw-up until she did get help. And now she's doing great. She's back at college full-time, acing all her courses. How else do you explain it?"

Slowly, Tony put down his knife and fork, shaking his head from side to side. And then, something I had never seen any of the Kenny men do, he burst out sobbing uncontrollably, bawling into his hands as he covered his face.

"I just can't believe it," he cried, "my own brother!"

I was on the verge of tears myself just watching this. The girlfriend tried to console him but he pushed her away. I was shocked at the effect my words had had on him. Clearly until I went logically over the sequence of events he had never considered that something like this could actually happen in his own family. He was now experiencing the same ontological meltdown as I had because this was indeed a truly devastating realization. He too had known Dad his whole life, his oldest brother, college graduate, engineer, businessman. And since he too was no stranger to infidelity that aspect of my father did not weigh on him so much, making this revelation not so much for him the worst of a series of them, but a single blow that now shattered his whole existence all at once.

On a fine sunny day the west coast of Ireland is truly a tonic for the soul and the following day the three of us set out on a drive west of Galway city on the coast road through Spiddle, then on across Connemara, with Galway Bay on the left, framed on the south by the coast of Clare that rises to become the Cliffs of Moher, and then beyond the mouth of the bay the long, low-lying ridges of rock that jut up out of the Atlantic to form the Aran Islands. Tony and I reminisced about the time two decades earlier that he had taken me there, flying out on a small plane, then back on the ferry. We had taken a horse and cart to Dun Aengus, a mysterious semi-circular stone fort whose missing half was said to have been shorn away to form Atlantis.

We stopped in Clifden for lunch and I reminded him that all those years ago he had treated this boy to his first ever steak in a restaurant. Tony now had four grown children of his own, but I was the oldest of all these cousins. I had returned to the Aran Islands years later using money he paid me to paint his house. We drove back inland, past the purple humps of The Twelve Bens, then along Lough Corrib. Tony fished here for salmon, and he golfed, and played squash, and in earlier days he had scuba-dived. He had a rifle and a shotgun and hunted pheasants and back when he lived in Dublin we would drive around and he would shoot sparrows roosting on the power lines. He once showed me how to eat raw periwinkles straight from the shell when we all went to The Coral Strand in Carraroe.

But now these memories could only be glimpsed through a veil that would be ever-present because of my words the previous night. Like me, Tony had now bitten the apple of knowledge and despite all this glorious nature that briefly buoyed our spirits he too was damned. The price of Mary's return to innocence, her salvation, her blossoming career, would continue to rise and would continue to be borne by those around her. We finished the day at Moran's Of The Weir, with oysters and Guinness, celebrating that time almost a decade earlier, when Tony had invited me, Kate, Mary and John to the Galway Oyster Festival for one last extravaganza of food and music before we took flight to the other side of this same Atlantic that we were looking out on now.

From there I drove back east again to stay with my oldest friend Colman who also now had a copy of my manuscript for the new novel. This threw even more cold water on my hopes for some encouragement, or even some enlightenment on what worked and what didn't in my narrative. I could not tell if he had even read the thing. He was fixated on the first page where I had used the word "elevator" which he insisted was never used in Ireland and that it should be "lift". Clearly, he derived no pleasure whatsoever either from my literary endeavour or my invitation to critique it.

I now had an appointment the following week with the publisher at Wolfhound Press, Seamus Cashman, and an invite from Steve and Geraldine to come and visit them in the meantime. Steve was an English professor at a college in Montana before they returned here and actually knew my all-time creative writing idol, John Gardner, whose *The Art Of Fiction* remains for me the best ever how-to book on the subject. We met at The Silken Thomas Bar in Kildare town, the only civilized eating and drinking establishment in this dreary conglomeration of stone ruins. I was going to spend the night with them, but they lived in a cottage in such a remote part of The Bog of Allen that it didn't have an address you could find on a map. I recognized Geraldine as soon as they walked into the bar, the long black hair, huge brown eyes, and freckles still unsubdued since childhood. She was taller than I remembered, in fact taller than her husband.

I bought her a white wine and Steve a lager and we launched straight into the subject of writing. They had returned to Ireland about a year earlier from Montana. Geraldine worked in the nearby town of Newbridge as an occupational therapist, and Steve at this point had despaired of actually finding employment of any kind as a writer and was trying to get a writer's magazine off the ground. I filled him in on my progress and my upcoming meeting. We ordered food and more drinks, then stocked up on beer and wine, and I followed their taillights along the pitch dark lanes that would have been impossible to navigate even in daylight.

Their home was indeed a small cottage with a slate roof. A living area took up the middle half and their bedroom was through a door that led to the other side of the fireplace. There was one more room at the opposite end of the house, which doubled as an office and spare bedroom. We chatted on for a while about Ireland and America and then Steve said he needed to crash because he had to drive to Wicklow early next day for a meeting. Geraldine refilled her wine glass indicating she had no intention of retiring so soon.

She talked a lot about my mother and about how kind she had been when she was growing up. It was then that I learned the extent of her father's binge drinking. He was a brilliant man, in fact he was the Chief Engineer for the Guinness brewing company. They had lived in Nigeria for a couple of years while he started up the brewery there, a sensational notion back when it happened, as if Black people drinking black beer was some kind of an oxymoron. Then he had invented the device that enabled Guinness draught in cans. Whatever the arrangement was with the company they paid him a lot of royalties or bonuses and he had given both of his daughters a chunk of their inheritance early and Geraldine had used hers to buy this house. I quizzed her about living in the middle of nowhere and got a lengthy lecture about the beauty of bogs and the importance of the biodiversity and how strip mining the peat needed to stop and about orchids and sedge grasses.

I had always thought of Geraldine as being shy, but now with a bottle or so of wine in her she was completely animated. And she had one of those lilting upper-class Dubin accents that was just a pleasure to listen to. Somehow the conversation came back to my mother and Geraldine lamented the travails she had been put through and declared that it was almost too much for a person to handle. And then the subject turned to me. She had gone out briefly with Michael though nothing came of it and she now told me that Michael had no chance living in my shadow. I was the golden-haired boy. I had it all.

This was getting a bit ridiculous so I told her I needed to get some sleep too and walked into the office cum bedroom. Geraldine followed me, wineglass in hand and asked if I needed anything. I assured her no and sat down on the bed. Then she closed the door, put down her glass, and sat down next to me. A minute later we were lying next to each other, kissing, while I groped for her breast. I sat bolt upright and pushed her away.

"Geraldine, this is insane! Steve is a few feet away. He could just walk in."

"He won't. He's a heavy sleeper."

"Don't you have work tomorrow?"

"I do, but I can get away early."

"I'll call you. Just go."

There was a hotel just outside Monasterevin, the next town south of Kildare. I booked a room and we met in the bar. Demure sober Geraldine was back. I asked was she sure. She rolled her eyes and shrugged. I picked up the room key and led the way. I have no idea how much time elapsed on that bed. Her shoulders were a constellation of freckles, her hair a wild black mane. There was nothing shy about her in bed. She moaned, gasped, panted, flailed her head from side to side, raised her knees, arched her back, dug her fingers into me, then climbed on top and rocked herself back and forth, over and over and over, more and more guttural grunts emanating from her until she just stopped and looked down at me, her long black tresses matted into her sweaty, reddened cheeks and said:

"Sean, if I come any more I'll die."

The day of the meeting came. I parked on Parnell Street and walked to 68 Mountjoy Square, the Georgian corner building that was the offices of Wolfhound Press. I was escorted up the two centuries old wooden staircase and straight into Cashman's office. He looked to be a few years older than me, with a full but neat beard. We shook hands and he sat down at his desk and I sat in one the chairs in front of it.

"How did you get here" he asked.

" I drove."

"Did you feed the meter?"

"I did."

"Good, good, because they're very quick to clamp wheels these days."

He then picked up a single sheet of paper and handed it to me. It was the reader report for my children's story. I read it quickly getting to the conclusion which was that this was a much better than average talking animal story and then the words: publish this.

"Wow, that's great," I said.

"Yeah," said Seamus, and then dug his hands into a box which I now saw contained the manuscript for The Ulstermen. "But what to do with this, I just don't know."

"I know," I said. It's way too long, but maybe..."

Before I could finish this thought, Seamus asked: "what are you working on now?"

And there it was. I told him about Garret O'Connor, whose brother was a well-known and notorious literary critic, and about Fionnula Flanagan and their workshop, and about the concept of trans-generational shame and how it had led me to come up with a present day businessman who inherits a small house in Mayo from his grand-aunt, goes over to see what this is about, gets drunk, tries to break in and tumbles over the half-door only to wake up in eighteen forty-five, the first year of The Great Famine. Here he encounters a starving family and becomes embroiled in their unfolding disaster. He returns to the present, where his cushy life begins to unravel, but is pulled back yet again, and this time matters are much worse. Some of the family are dead and the rest evicted. Now he gets fully involved but falls in with a marauding gang only to find that they are cannibals. This time he returns to wake up in a lunatic asylum but eventually recovers and moves into the house. He tries to piece together the whole thing only to discover that he himself is directly descended from the head cannibal.

"How long is this one?" asked Seamus.

"About sixty thousand words."

"Get that in to me right away."

"I'll drop it off tomorrow."

Push had become pull, a far, far better situation for the writer. This was nineteen ninety four, and if it was to be published in nineteen ninety-five, the one hundred and fiftieth anniversary of the Great Famine, it needed to get into the publishing queue immediately. I drove to Drogheda, stayed the night with Colman, tied one on with him in Clark's, another legendary watering hole unsullied by any post-war modernization. I retrieved my precious though unappreciated manuscript, and dropped it off as promised.

The pressure was off now and I still had several days before my return flight, which would have been expensive to change. I drove south to meet Geraldine in The Woodenbridge Hotel for more sex, wine, and laughter. On our last day together she showed up in a plunging blouse wearing far more perfume than usual. Would we see each other again? I said I didn't know but I would set up a PO box and write to her at her office. She teared up, we hugged and kissed, I brought the car back to Kate's brother, and took a taxi to Dublin Airport

Chapter Fifteen. 1995 - 1998

◇ Welcome to the Hotel California

Such a lovely place, such a lovely face
They're livin' it up at the Hotel California

What a nice surprise, bring your alibis ◇

The Eagles

I now returned one more time to my old company, this time to manage a swords-to-plough-shares exercise. We had developed a very accurate sensor to control the fuel flow into the engines of the stealth bomber, one that maximised its range and would be impervious to the nuclear pulse after it dropped the bomb on Moscow, but the Cold War was over and we were now permitted to sell these to anyone anywhere. We sold some to the Chinese and to the oil industry in Canada, they were already now standard on civilian airliners too.

I exchanged a few letters with Geraldine but this just aggravated my feelings of self-loathing so I soon stopped. What I had done was bad enough, but at least my wife was on the other side of the world and not in the next room. And however beautiful and desirable she was did I really want to run off with a woman who was so casual about all this? Would she cheat on me with some new guy that came along? Moreover my two kids were still not old enough to be self-sufficient, there was no way Kate would let me have them anyway, and she could not look after them on her own.

The contract duly arrived for my famine book, whose title was now *The Hungry Earth* and by this time like millions of American homes we had a fax machine, so the planning and editing process had suddenly become much easier. My editor, Adrienne Murphy, did a terrific job on both the text and the cover blurb. And then my old friend, Joe O'Sullivan, from my days in Cork came to visit. He had moved across town to a better job with Apple Computer and had then taken up an assignment in Tokyo managing key suppliers from there. But now he was being tapped to come to the corporate headquarters to head up a new supply chain function called 'outsourcing'. And he wanted me to come and join him.

I flew to San Jose and did a round of interviews, totally overdressed on a campus where everyone wore shorts, sandals and Hawaiian shirts, or whatever they liked. This would be a fresh start for all of us. But Joe himself was not going to relocate his family until the end of the school year, which gave me time to wind up my job, then fly to Ireland for the launch of *The Hungry Earth*. I did see Geraldine, but just for the purpose of making sure we both knew this was over, and over permanently. I didn't detect any remorse on her part, but then almost a year had now elapsed. She showed me her new herd of goats, told me all their names, and we parted on good terms.

The publicist at Wolfhound at that time was a brilliant young woman called Ciara Considine, herself the daughter of a novelist, and who would go on to head up Penguin Books in Ireland. She had lined up a series of interviews, of which by far the most important was a thirty-minute slot on The Pat Kenny Show - no relation - which was the most popular daytime talk radio show and which single-handedly got my name out to the whole country. But she also lined up days of other radio interviews, and a TV slot in Cork. Then, over the coming months the book was reviewed positively in over a dozen newspapers, many that I had never heard of, and every bookshop in Ireland was stocked with a few copies.

On the one hand I was naturally very excited about all of this, it was my life-long dream come true, but on the flight over I had been filled with trepidation. The famine was, after all, Ireland's Holocaust. Between one and two million people perished and the mass emigration that followed cut the population in half and it had never recovered. They didn't die of starvation as I had once thought, because they didn't live long enough. They succumbed to various diseases with which they all infected each other. The cover image that Wolfhound had chosen was a painting by Ireland's most famous impressionist painter, Jack Yeats, brother of the poet. The original was, and is, in the collection in a room in the K Club of most of his work and it is a fitting image, one of a haunted-looking old man alone in a wild barren landscape under dark clouds, somewhere in the west of Ireland, a person beyond all hope.

Was it right for me to mine this almost unimaginable tragedy to achieve my years-long goal? Apparently it was or at least no one has ever suggested that it wasn't. And it obviously dovetailed with Garret O'Connor's ideas about trans-generational shame. The Irish were a conquered people as yet incapable of lifting themselves out of their national inferiority complex and just about every reviewer agreed that my successful time slip sequences between present- day materialism and the enormous suffering of the famine had shone a spotlight on the Irish psyche. Whatever other personal issues still dogged me, I returned home vindicated that I really could write a novel.

I commuted for a while to Cupertino, to Apple's headquarters and traveled around the area as time allowed. This job would involve almost continuous travel so a lengthy drive to work would not be that intolerable. We rented a house a stone's throw from the beach in the seaside town of Aptos, toward the north end of Monterey Bay. Santa Cruz, surf city itself, was fifteen minutes up the coast, while Monterey, with its famed Cannery Row and aquarium was a half hour to the south. I knew I was wrenching my kids away from their friends and into new schools just as they were entering adolescence and hoped that the excitement of living by the sea would somewhat compensate for this.

At this time Apple was at the nadir of its fortunes. An enormous industry of clones had emerged in which dozens of companies simply combined an Intel microprocessor with the Microsoft Windows operating system. I owned one of these, which I bought at a computer fair where vendors would vie with each other to assemble a personal computer to your specifications right in front of you. Apple's revenue was overwhelmingly from the sale of desktop Macs, and their global market share of this segment had fallen into the single digits. The solution was obvious - you only had to look at the other leading brands, HP and Dell, to see that they had nothing to do with manufacturing the hardware, which they outsourced to rapidly growing EMS companies - electronic manufacturing services providers. But implementing this at Apple meant dismantling their touchy- feely culture, at least as far as their factories were concerned.

Seamus Cashman contacted me to tell me that I should attend the upcoming San Francisco Book Fair because they were going to have a writer's panel with the theme of The Irish Famine and they wanted me as a speaker. He was sending over some of my books. I now had one important fan in the USA, California State Senator Tom Hayden. He had bought the book while part of a delegation to Belfast, where The Troubles still raged on, then tracked me down. Tom was a famous anti-war protester back in the sixties, now an ardent environmentalist, and was famously married to the actress Jane Fonda at one point. He wanted me to contribute an essay for an anthology he was working on exploring the Irish psyche and his own Irish roots, and he too would be speaking. We met at the Book Fair along with various other writers and the actor Gabriel Byrne, who also spoke, talking about the money the Choctaw tribe had raised at the time to help the starving Irish. Then he signed autographs for a long line of fans, we all went to some dinner hosted by the Democratic Party, made our way to an Irish bar off North Beach that was, and still is, decorated with murals of various Irish writers, where some woman literally pulled me off my bar stool so she could sit next to Gabriel.

Per Seamus' instructions I sought out the publisher Roberts-Rinehart at the fair and introduced myself. A month later Seamus faxed me to say they wanted to publish my book in hardback in the USA. And soon after that a couple of Hollywood producers optioned *The Hungry Earth*. On the strength of all this Seamus told me I should get started on a follow-up novel in the same genre. Then, nineteen ninety-five gave way to nineteen ninety-six and I filled up a notebook with ideas and cluster diagrams. But now I was being pulled in all directions. My parents came to visit and even they commented that something would have to give. It was the first time I had seen them since they had reunited and Dad certainly was on his best behaviour, but then why would he not be now that he had prevailed yet again?

The house we had rented was a two story upside-down house, with a wrap-around deck outside the upper floor. The front door was at the top of a staircase and led into the main living area, with the master bedroom off to one side. Downstairs had more bedrooms and a room I used as my office. Kate insisted she could handle the stairs but I could see it was gradually becoming more difficult for her. Once inside she could get around with her cane well enough and the two kids were now old enough to be of great help to her when I was traveling. I kept asking myself would things be different between us if she was in better health and I would think about it drinking beer on the deck or walking along the beach and out along the pier that led to the old concrete tanker that had once been a speakeasy until it sank in a storm. Now it was a sea lion colony.

Kate and I had known each other for over a quarter of a century and we had grown and changed along the way. I often wondered if her condition was not a consequence in some way of her own terrible childhood. She was the oldest and the apple of her father's eye. He used to tell her that he never wanted any of the others, her four sisters and her brother. He was abusive to her mother and she had seen him bash in the bedroom door one time when she locked it and fling her down the stairs naked. She had sat across the table as her mother told her she was going to kill herself and swallowed a handful of sleeping pills. They never celebrated hers or any of the others' birthdays.

She had been a fashion maven since I first met her and would spend days shopping for the perfect pair of boots, or the latest batwing top or padded shoulder jacket. Her hair was always a work in progress going from perm to straight to pageboy and she was very fastidious about her eye make-up and how everything had to match. I did most of the cooking but she had her own recipes too - lasagne, pesto, chili. When I first introduced her as my fiancée to one of my mother's friends, Maureen Donegan, she observed that she could see the attraction, that there was a serenity about Kate that was very special. My own view was that this was a defence mechanism, an aura of don't-get-too-close, although of course it had the opposite effect. There was no shortage of beautiful women at Apple, but I had learned my lesson. It would have to be one or the other.

The Hungry Earth had grown out of a great idea that explained the sorry state of the Ireland I had grown up in but its protagonist was really a metaphor for all that was wrong with it whereas this new story was more deeply personal. I now had my own self-loathing to deal with and I needed a character who was flawed himself in a way that would bring him down. This would be a story about hubris, my way of atoning for what I had done with Geraldine. My parents' visit had caused me to cast my mind back to their visit to Kinsale and that in turn got me thinking about moving statues and sacred sites in general. What if an American screenwriter moves to the west of Ireland with his Irish actress wife where her brother still runs the family farm just outside a small village on the coast? They buy a site to build their dream home, on top of a hill with spectacular views, but first they have to bulldoze away a stone circle, what the locals called a fairy rath. What if there really was something to all this moving statue malarkey? Christianity was an imported religion so how much more power would the ancient indigenous beliefs wield?

Moreover I could work the whole father-daughter incest theme in here. The story is set eighteen years in the past and he is recounting it today. As they are building the house his wife becomes pregnant. Then he encounters an astonishingly beautiful girl walking along the beach and they become lovers. The ever- rising tide of catastrophes ends with the house being burned down, by a character based on Kate, but the baby survives while the mother is immolated. Cut back to the present and in the very last scene this now eighteen- year-old girl walks in the door and it is the same girl he had sex with all those years earlier. I would have to take a leave of absence from Apple but we had now reached a point where we would need to let the dust settle on the American factory sell-offs anyway, the lowest-hanging fruit, before tackling the rest of it.

Justin and Helen had settled in and made new friends. Justin joined junior lifeguards and began to learn to surf. Helen was more interested in the music scene in Santa Cruz and was taking an interest in drama. Justin had discovered that on his way to the bus stop he could duck into the local motel and help himself to pastries. Helen read my children's novel which she said made her cry because too many birds die in it. Mom began calling more frequently to say Dad was drinking a half bottle of whiskey a day again and hardly spoke to her and when he did he kept accusing her of being disloyal to him, and I was left to assure her again that it was the other way around and always had been. It was unbearable how he was causing her to feel remorse for leaving him and felt none himself for any of the deeds that had led up to it. And though we did not know it at the time even darker storm clouds were gathering back east.

In nineteen-ninety-seven John and Mary bought a house in the affluent town of Yorktown Heights, about fifty miles up The Hudson River Valley from New York City. Rex was now seventeen and Layla was fourteen. Mary was finishing her sociology post-graduate degree and was working at a centre for abused women nearby. John had started his own business the previous year and that was going well and on the surface they were living the American dream but all that soon unraveled. Layla began spending her days in her bedroom with her seventeen-year-old drug dealing boyfriend, over John's vehement objections which were not shared by Mary. Rex too was getting up to mischief which went largely unnoticed because it paled in comparison to what Layla was doing. John fretted about this obvious lack of supervision but Mary took the position that he was just jealous of his kids and was behaving like his own maniacal father.

In early nineteen ninety-eight Mary unilaterally made the decision that Kevin and Anne were coming to live with them over John's strenuous objections. As he saw it they were already having enough issues with their kids and having other people living there would only add to the mayhem. Mary shrugged him off declaring, "tough shit, they're on their way". As John saw it their sex life was already on the rocks and having another couple under their roof would complicate any hope of ever rekindling it. Kevin and Anne moved in, picked up jobs at a local bar, worked till after midnight, then sat around smoking and drinking into the small hours.

A couple of months later, Mary informed John that Finbarr was coming back to America from Ireland and was also going to live with them for a while until he got his own place, further amplifying the late night mayhem. Finbarr got a job soon enough, but barely managed to make it to work three days a week out of five. He was depressed and angry about his life and joined in the late night drinking and toking pot every night of the week. Layla was a welcome participant in her uncle and aunt's revelry, claiming she couldn't sleep and chain-smoking her nights away with them. On top of that she kept insisting that her soon-to-be-jailbird boyfriend should also be allowed to move in which added to the nightly consternation.

Matters then went from bad to worse. John and Mary received word from the high school that three girls in Layla's year were pregnant as a result of drug-fuelled orgies at a local motel. On questioning, Layla admitted to being there too. There were three dealers involved, her boyfriend and two others, one of whom would soon die of an overdose. The girls were doing pot laced with roofies and then being date raped. To pay for their drugs they were required to help steal property in some cases from their own homes, that could be hauled down to the New York City and bartered for more drugs. Or, they could become dealers themselves and sell to their high school friends. Rex also wanted in on this easy money and was soon arrested for stealing a postal scale from Walmart.

Layla assured Mary she would stop going to the motel, but she didn't. Eventually John, at his wits end, warned her he would physically hit her if she continued. A bruised daughter was far preferable to a dead one and when Layla persisted and John did whack her the upshot from Mary and Anne was that he was the abuser and she was the victim. Layla was then arrested for dealing, bailed out by her parents and then arrested again. They warned her they would not bail her out a third time but lo and behold she was arrested again and, without consulting John, Mary posted bail yet again.

Eventually, the situation with Layla became so bad that they packed her up and drove her the two hours east to her grandparents. This decision mystified Kate and I. How could any mother send their teenage daughter to live with the man she had emphatically accused, in writing, of childhood sexual abuse? Was this some bizarre experiment to see if Dad would now somehow atone for what he had done? Mary, to this day has not recanted the statement that she was raped by her father as a young child. And what about John and Finbarr and Anne? They either must not believe Mary or have convinced themselves that a woke Mom would stand in the way of any further shenanigans or that the old bastard had long since chemically castrated himself with Irish whiskey.

Chapter Sixteen. 1998

And who could play it well enough
If deaf and dumb and blind with love?
He that made this knows all the cost
For he gave all his heart and lost.

William Butler Yeats

Back at Apple we now took on the divestiture of the Singapore manufacturing operation. I spent months living out of the Hyatt Hotel, eating dinner at one of the chic restaurants on Boat Quay or in the cloister of a repurposed convent, or sometimes just nasi goreng served on banana leaves, in noisy food courts, where roasted ducks dangled from hooks above the vendors. I signed up for scuba diving lessons. On the weekends we would drive over the causeway to Johore Bharu in a minivan, then up the east coast of Malaysia to sleep rough on a fishing boat that took us out to small islands in the South China Sea. We dived on blue spotted sting rays and huge sea cucumbers. Venomous stone fish and lion fish lurked at the bases of the brain corals where white and orange striped clown fish darted about and the occasional moray eel slid from one cave to another.

On one of my trips home from Asia I routed myself back through Ireland to do the publicity tour for *Celtic Fury,* as they had finally named my follow-up to *The Hungry Earth.* Ciara had now moved on, and this new publicist was no match. The book itself was gorgeous with a muted nude on the cover which spoke to the core of the story. Inside was a page of quotes from reviews of *The Hungry Earth,* all taken from a file of meticulously collected clippings of various reviews, including now the ones from American reviews. But I was no longer a new talent bursting onto the Irish literary scene and this novel's only hook was its connection to my previous one and not the anniversary of Ireland's greatest calamity. Hardly a dog barked.

We wrapped up the Singapore business with a deal that gave Natsteel, a publicly quoted Singapore company, all of the assets plus a contract to make a billion dollars of motherboards on these machines for us. I returned to Cupertino glad to be back with my family. We moved from the upside-down house to a single-story rental in Capitola, the jewel in the crown of California's seaside villages that lay between Aptos and Santa Cruz. It was a few minutes' walk from this house to the tall railroad trestle bridge that spans the Soquel river below and overlooks Capitola pier and the crescent of bars and restaurants along the waterfront. To the left you could see the old concrete tanker and almost make out our old house while to the right a row of jagged cliffs separated us first from Santa Cruz Harbour and then further on from Santa Cruz boardwalk with its historic roller coaster.

These long absences were steadily pushing Kate and I further apart. Given her condition she was entitled to claim permanent disability and for a while she did. But she loved nursing, and she knew from the time I met her when she was fifteen that this would be her career. When she came back to Dublin she had been low woman on the totem pole and was assigned to the geriatric ward to watch old men sitting on their deathbeds smoking cigarettes. Disillusioned, she briefly quit to study marketing but she soon found a much better nursing job in a cardiac unit. Now she had found a nursing job in Santa Cruz in a post-surgical rehab unit. Hers was a linear path through life whereas mine was this crazy zig-zag.

On top of that I now hated my job at Apple. Back in Cupertino I was again accumulating staff and overseeing the microprocessor and memory chip supply chain. My fortieth birthday came and Kate and the kids treated me to a paragliding adventure off Santa Cruz wharf. But even soaring over Monterey Bay failed to lift my spirits. If my life was a three-legged stool, two of them were now broken. My marriage was now no more than two intelligent, considerate people sharing a home together and being polite to each other for the sake of the two children they loved. But these children were now confident American teenagers and Justin would have a driving permit within the year. Ireland was a receding memory and after ten years in America we had not the slightest intention of returning there so whatever glue that had brought to our marriage no longer held.

The one aspect of my life that now seemed solid was my writing. I had three titles in every book shop in Ireland and a hardback copy of *The Hungry Earth* in every bookstore in America. I knew this because I was always checking. It was in The Santa Cruz Bookstore. It was in Capitola Book Cafe. When I drove around at lunch time I found it in Borders, in

Crown Books, in Barnes and Noble. They had sold it to libraries and it had made its way onto a couple of college courses. I had been interviewed on NPR - National Public Radio - and had been positively reviewed in Publishers Weekly, which reviewed everything. The various local Irish American newspapers had covered it and it was now in development as a script at HBO. *Celtic Fury* was optioned by a British film production company.

This was in reality the high-water mark of my writing career though I did not yet know it. Not that it was over, and Seamus Cashman was receptive to adding more novels to my list, but there would never be a point again when so much was happening at once. We booked a vacation in Cozumel to give ourselves something to look forward to, but even that did not allay my fears about my own long-term future. I was heading into my middle years in a dying marriage that I could not resuscitate and I was terrified to act. We had married very young and I was not sure whether I could competently live on my own at all.

I would not be setting a family precedent if I left Kate. Of the four of us who were now married, Michael had already left Jackie. The last time we had seen them was when we had rendezvoused in Santa Fé. They had flown from Dallas and we had driven from Redlands. They had said they would drive so we had built a small model railroad for Adam, who was then two, and ended up bringing it back again. Michael had said he would arrange to pick it up but he never did and we gave it to the kid next door when we moved north. Jackie told us in Santa Fe that she was again pregnant and in due course gave birth to a baby girl, Megan.

I only have Jackie's version of what happened but apparently Michael had a complete breakdown in the hospital. Whether it was because they had kept the gender secret or the full realization that he now had a daughter he declared, presumably in a drunken rage, that he could not possibly raise a girl because he might be a pedophile like his father and stormed out and just disappeared. He resurfaced in Turkey for a while and then moved to Johannesburg. I tried to talk to him but he was not interested. For a long time I wondered how he could look himself in the mirror but how dissimilar was what I was now contemplating?

I left both Apple and Kate and both were very messy affairs. Things were still bleak at Apple and executives were bailing left and right but Steve Jobs had returned and his hands- on management style was already becoming apparent. I had e-mailed him about a bigger role in operations and he had asked me what were my ideas. I sent another e-mail with a suggested reorganization but after not hearing back for a few weeks I accepted a job with Natsteel to head up their US operations. This incensed Jobs both because I had left and because he knew I had been the point person in the huge Singapore outsourcing deal and felt that what I was doing was unethical. Fortunately I was well-regarded in the Apple legal department and they convinced him I had done nothing wrong.

I told Kate about my affair in the hope she would kick me out. Instead, while I was at work the next day she called Geraldine and had it out with her. Apparently Geraldine apologized profusely and assured Kate that she was the one who had started it and that I had ended it. But I had now crossed this Rubicon. I had to tell Kate that our marriage had grown flat and that I felt it was best for both of us if we separated now while we were still young enough to possibly make a fresh start. She asked was there someone else and I do not know if she believed me when I told her no, but there wasn't. I desperately did not want her to feel the stigma of rejection and tried every variation of the old it's not you it's me argument.

Kate was still the same person she had always been. She was a beautiful, kind, gentle woman and always would be. I on the other hand had now completely reinvented myself, which I had felt compelled to do so as not to end up in an asylum, or prison, or worse. And I could not now put the genie back in the bottle. I can't say how much better of a person I was, but I was very different. I had learned at a workshop years earlier the phrase "we write to right our lives" and it always stayed with me. Although I had found an outlet for all the conflict in me I was still very conflicted and always would be. I was well along the road on a journey of personal growth but I still had more work to do and the old me that Kate had married no longer existed.

We all agreed we were going to go ahead with our Mexico vacation in a few weeks time, which we did. Kate even got to go scuba diving with a divemaster who held her hand the whole time. Justin had his life-long love of reptiles rewarded when he was allowed to handle an alligator, muzzled of course, and Helen had her life-long love of dolphins even more gratified by swimming in a pool with a pair of them so friendly they danced for her and lay quietly next to her while she petted them. It was the perfect transition and even though I had moved out they knew I would never be far away. Helen still remembers the night I left because she came back from a Reel Big Fish And The Aquabats ska punk concert in Santa Cruz to find me gone.

Monterey Bay is separated from Silicon Valley by a range of heavily wooded mountains and I bought a condominium over the hill in the town of Saratoga about twenty miles away. I also helped to buy Kate and the kids a house in Aptos that was perfect for them. It had a vaulted ceiling over the living room with a downstairs master bedroom and two upstairs ones with their own bathroom. Life went on as before and Justin even remarked that now they were just like all their friends who all had divorced parents too. We had not quite reached that point but Kate soon started seeing someone. He devised a sling for his yacht to get her on and off and took her sailing in the bay. He played the guitar and the kids liked him and he also had a couple of kids close to their ages.

Natsteel's US activities were two-fold, one was business development, looking for new customers, and more importantly new business from existing customers. This invariably came from new products always being brought out by IBM, HP, Compaq, and a few start-ups. The other was new product introduction, or rapid prototyping as it was also called. We would prove out the designs at our little factory in Silicon Valley and then ramp the volume production in Asia or Mexico. My first task was to consolidate us from the two overcrowded facilities that we rented in San Jose and that search led us to a facility in Morgan Hill, a commuter town about ten miles south of the sprawling south bay metropolis, separated from it by a green belt called Coyote Valley. This was a Singaporean company and I was now its highest- ranking Caucasian employee. The others were ethnically Chinese who took matters of fengshui very seriously so we made some alterations at our new location, such as ensuring my door did not look out on the street as that could cause all our money to flee, and petitioning the city to change our street number to all ascending digits.

As nineteen ninety-seven drew to a close we held our work holiday party at a nearby hotel. Most of the staff brought significant others, but one of our

PAs, the people responsible for the minutiae of the product builds, seemed to be alone, so I asked if we could sit together. Peg Fordney was a vivacious girl from the East Coast, with long black hair, and a penchant for Chardonnay. As the night wore on we both opened up to each other. She had come to Silicon Valley with her engineer husband and two young children, but it was her third relocation, and she had had enough. She was going through a rough divorce and her only friend was another mother with kids at the same daycare. She hated the fact that she was the one who had to move out and all she could afford was a single room, which made it difficult to see her children, Kelly and Charlie.

My job saw me mostly on the road, visiting customers in Texas, Colorado, Boston, Toronto, or taking them to Mexico or Singapore, but in the new year Peg and I started to see more of each other. She remained distraught over her marriage and against the advice of her lawyer refused to ask for alimony or even child support. Sometimes when I dropped her off at her digs we would sit in the car and she would sob. I wasn't sure what to make of this and questioned whether this was just a rebound thing but as things progressed and she started staying over at my place her wicked sense of humour came to the fore and before long she was hanging her clothes in my wardrobe.

Meanwhile Kate and her new boyfriend went on sailing charter trips to The Virgin Islands and New Zealand. She asked me for a divorce, which was a huge relief, and we both went to a mediator and told him that I wanted nothing, she could have the house, and I would help out with any costs for Justin and Helen until they left home. We paid the mediator three hundred dollars and soon after that I signed the house over to her and her boyfriend moved in. Justin joined the high school snowboarding club and Helen joined junior theatre. Peg finalized her divorce with a strict fifty-fifty custody arrangement and the proviso that neither she nor her husband could move more than thirty miles away.

The changes in Peg were now amazing. At my suggestion she took scuba-diving lessons in Monterey, in preparation for a trip to the Caribbean. She had intended to go alone to Antigua, but I persuaded her to let me meet up with her, did some research and settled on going on to a tiny Dutch island called Saba, which has superb diving on underwater sea-mounts, which we did and swam with shoals of barracuda and scared up some stingrays buried in the sand. We stayed at a guest house called Mister Cranston's, where the owner just served whatever fish he had on hand that day for dinner, then we spent a couple of days on Saint Kitt's where we did a wreck dive in the harbour, took a taxi around the island to see the old sugar plantations, and ate out in a bit more style.

Peg changed up her hair style to a short bob, which accentuated her luminous smile and, as I would always tell her, she had the best lips on any white woman. Every second weekend when she did not have Kelly and Charlie we would just take off on a road trip with a spontaneity she had never experienced before and which delighted her. I painted her toenails poolside at The Highland Inn above Carmel, we drove south past Big Sur to tour Hearst Castle and stayed at the beach at Cambria, we kayaked Morro Bay across the oyster beds, we drove north to Bodega Bay, and went wine tasting up and down The Russian River, we went to Napa and did the mud baths at Calistoga. The sun shone and there wasn't a cloud in the sky.

Chapter Seventeen. 1998 - 1999.

And may her bridegroom bring her to a house
Where all's accustomed, ceremonious;
For arrogance and hatred are the wares
Peddled in the thoroughfares.

William Butler Yeats

When Peg first arrived in California she set about looking for a job as a bookkeeper. She literally knocked on the door of every business in the neighbourhood. When she got to Natsteel the finance person interviewed her on the spot. They didn't need anyone in accounting but would she be interested in being a Program Administrator? Peg said she was willing to give it a try, was hired and quickly learned the job from the other PAs. When I arrived it didn't take long to realize that she was wasted in that role and I moved her to the business development team, never mind that she was now my girlfriend and this meant a fifty percent pay increase.

Then, in the summer of nineteen ninety-eight, Apple descended en masse on our new facility. Steve Jobs had sent them to order me to start building the prototype motherboards for their new product immediately. This was a tear-drop shaped all-in-one machine, reminiscent of the original Mac, but with a translucent housing that came in different colours. Jobs was betting the company on this machine, the iMac. Because of its curved housing the motherboards were not the usual rectangles, but an irregular polygon, making it a new challenge to move them through our machines and to build the test fixtures.

Apple's cult of secrecy was fully in place and anyone who leaked any information about future products was instantly dismissed. Their team brought the bare boards, microprocessors and custom chips with them and we commenced the usual matrix experiments to see what vendors parts worked together. Of the first run of one hundred boards we got a handful to pass test. We did a second run based on these and the yield went up a bit. But now with the launch deadline fast approaching we began to work around the clock. We were in Morgan Hill and the assembly plant was in Sacramento, about a three hour drive away. To shorten that transfer time I charted a small plane and pilot at a nearby private airport. Once we had a dozen or so working boards we had our driver grab the totes and rush them to the plane where the pilot had been alerted to have the engine running and he flew them to an airport near the factory where an Apple driver rushed them to the assembly line.

The motherboards were dropped into the housings and the drives and keyboards were plugged in. Apple's engineers figured out what worked, what didn't and why. They then e-mailed us an updated bill of materials, but that was all they shared with us. We then printed this out and two PA's sat side by side with steel rules and highlighters and compared the old and new. They then told us what parts had been changed, one of them ran to the parts cage to get the new value capacitors and resistors and the other ran to the chip shooter to tell the techs which reels of parts were about to be replaced.

We went through iteration after iteration of this until we finally got the yield close to ninety-percent. Singapore was told to ramp production and in August the product that would forever change Apple was launched. There were billboards everywhere showing a smiling Steve Jobs holding an iMac by the carry handle integrated into the back of the monitor. I was now a made man at Natsteel, but they were now all too aware of my relationship with Peg. This was not a big deal with my Asian management who saw nothing wrong with screwing the hired help but it troubled Peg and she began looking around for another job.

She was soon hired by an even bigger contract manufacturer with another big pay increase in the role of Global Account Manager. Although we had bought bunk beds for her kids my condominium had nowhere for them to play or ride bikes, so we sold it and rented a house in San Jose, not far from where their father lived. We debated whether I should just quit because we could live off her salary now and certainly in this hectic work environment it was impossible to get any writing done. Seamus had told me to keep going but I did in fact have a manuscript called *The King Snake* ready to go. Peg had read it and made a few good suggestions so I was not really under a lot of pressure to crank out yet another one for now.

Then earth-shattering news arrived. My mother had been diagnosed with bowel cancer and would have to undergo surgery immediately. I flew east to join Dad, Mary, John, Finbarr and Anne at her bedside. The operation had saved her life for now, but she had only months to live. As it happened Peg was visiting a customer in Boston at the same time and this was now her introduction to my family, Mom lying semi-conscious on the bed surrounded by the others. Dad's very first comment to, or rather about, Peg was:

"Sure, aren't all American women cute hoors."

One of the few coherent things Mom said before she dozed off was:

"Sean, you know you never see grapes for sale in American hospitals. Isn't that odd?"

We all left except Dad, and Peg and I went on a search for grapes which took us a while because Hartford was mostly shut down on a Sunday. We found some and went back to the hospital. Dad was still sitting there, dozing off himself until I walked in.

"Wha? Wha? What's that?" he asked.

"She said she wanted grapes."

He made a loud snorting noise, threw his head back, and rolled his eyes.

"She can't eat bloody grapes!" he shouted.

I put the grapes down on her tray and walked out. We drove to The Cracker Barrel to meet the others and share a few pitchers of beer. Mary said she would host a big Christmas for everyone and I said I would bring Justin and Helen. We all knew that my mother's entire life centred around planning the next big event. Back in Ireland she would have already made the Christmas cakes and puddings. The planning for Easter started on Ash Wednesday. And summer never went by without going away somewhere, be that Spain, Kerry, West Cork, Dromineer on Lough Derg, Passage East, Sligo, or down the Grand Canal in a cabin cruiser. So many great memories of so many great times she had given us, and now there would be no more. Of course we would give her this to look forward to. Michael even said he would fly up from South Africa.

The entire family had migrated to America, but not at the same time and not in the same way. Dad and Mom had leveraged a business relationship and had brought Michael, Finbarr and Anne across to initially live with them. Jackie followed Michael and married him but both John and I had made our way here independently in pursuit of career opportunities. John was a talented software developer and a fearless entrepreneur. By this time he had established a successful business and he, Mary, Rex and Layla were living their best lives in a huge home in Westchester County, New York City's most prestigious suburb, or so we thought. I would not become aware of the drug related shenanigans I have recounted earlier until many years later. When I arrived with Justin and Helen I was very impressed with the decor, a far cry from the various rental dumps they had lived in over the years. The living room was dominated by a huge black and white portrait of the four of them taken by John's youngest sister, who was now a professional photographer. It was a fitting symbol for all that they had accomplished.

Mom lay propped up on a couch, clearly delighted to see us all, but just as clearly struggling with the pain any time she moved. Dad mooched around muttering about her MuMu. Could we not persuade her to wear a girdle? We hiked to the top of the hill behind the house - Dad, me, Justin, Helen, Rex, John, Mary, Finbarr, Anne. Kevin was already busy in the kitchen and Layla was not there. I was still unclear what my mother's exact prognosis was but no-one was willing to enlighten me. We ate dinner, cleared up, then gathered in the big family room for a game of Global Pursuit. This was the same game we had played seven years earlier in Bar Harbor using five-sided tiles to form an expanding floor puzzle with players scoring based on their answers to geographical questions. Helen was now fourteen, still the youngest, so we had her ask the questions.

Mom watched from her couch. Dad participated and uncannily repeated his bizarre behaviour from back then, making Helen repeat every question as though she had not read it out right the first time, and then when he could not come up with the correct answer accusing her of being wrong. Helen was the sunniest girl in the world and indulged him every time and it was all I could do not to yell at her to stop encouraging him but why spoil the fun for everyone else. We wrapped up the game playing and the kids went to bed to get up early and go snowboarding. Mary and Anne helped Mom up the stairs then came back and we all hung about smoking and drinking until the conversation turned to the plane tickets to Ireland.

"There won't be time for any of this nonsense," Dad declared.

"Why not?" asked Anne.

"She wants to see her old friends," added Mary.

"What friends?" Dad asked.

"You know," said Mary.

"No I bloody don't. Make a list of them."

"For god's sake," said Anne.

"The bigger point," I interjected, "is that we have to give her something to look forward to."

"For the love of god," said Dad, "she's dying of cancer."

"Yes, and we want to do everything we can for her in the time she has left." I was starting to lose it with him, but he beat me to it.

"I'm sensing a lot of hostility from this whole family. You're all a bunch of useless fucking shitheads." He picked up a wicker chair next to the one he was sitting on and banged it up and down. "Don't any of you shed any shagging crocodile tears for me when I die!"

"Johnny, this is not about you," said John.

"What? Bejesus it certainly is. Mary's letter is what tore this whole family apart and probably gave her mother cancer."

"That's bullshit!" I shouted. "You're the one who wrecked the lives of everyone around you. And this didn't start now. It goes way back."

"What did I ever do to you," he retorted. "The only thing you've ever had to complain about is that you had to take two buses to school."

"There's nothing new here," I replied. "You've wrecked every Christmas all our lives and now here you are doing it again."

"What? Sure you and Kate couldn't even look me in the eye!"

"It's the other way around. The last time Kate saw you was Anne and Kevin's wedding and she saw right through you one last time."

"Well I want absolutely nothing from anyone accusing me of being a serial rapist."

"You're accusing my wife of being a liar," shouted John, "you're abusing her right now and I will not stand by ever again and let you do that. You're not in control here."

"What? Of course I'm in control. She is my wife of forty-three years and I am the one looking after her now with no help from any of you and I've had enough of it."

"That's fine with me," I said. "I'll quit my job and take care of her full time. You're the cause of her illness. You subjected her to chronic stress from day one of those forty-three years and now she is just shutting down because she is imprisoned in a relationship with you with no hope of escape."

"Bloody nonsense! What have you ever done for me anyway?"

"I worked for you for five years."

"You did nothing for me."

"And when I was of no further use to you, you threw me aside and moved on to your next big thing. You are a rapist," I shouted. "And Mary tried to kill herself because of it when she was eighteen. It's taken us all years of therapy of all sorts to get past it all."

"It's pretty obvious some kind of abuse went on," John interjected, gesturing to Mary. "She's turned her life around, put herself through college and now she helps other women damaged by the likes of you."

"You don't have to take care of Mom," said Anne to Dad. "We all will. Gladly."

He banged the wicker chair up and down again. "Well then go ahead, because I've had enough of it all, you shower of bloody wasters!"

He stood up and walked out of the room with that forced marching gait he put on when he was angry. After a minute, we heard the bedroom door banging. At some point in all this Finbarr had left as he usually did when a row like this started. Next morning we all woke up to find that Dad was gone. He had said nothing to Mom about why he was leaving or when or if he would be back. The following day he had still not reappeared but I had to fly back with Justin and Helen. Michael and I passed like ships in the night, which left me with mixed feelings, but I heard he too was very distressed, drank heavily, and warned everyone that he would kill the next person who said we were a dysfunctional family.

A few days later Dad sent an e-mail to all of us, reversing his position and stating that he alone was in control of Mom's care and telling us that if we wanted to change that situation we should contact their lawyers and giving us said law firm's address. He also said that there was to be no communication with her except through him and that he would not hesitate to call the police if any of us showed up unexpectedly at the door. He didn't carry through on that but he would not answer the door to Kevin after they brought Mom home, nor answer the phone to Anne. I called on New Year's Day and he did answer, but told me Mom was asleep. I asked him to wish her a happy new year from me which he said he would do, but he didn't. Mom later told Anne that she was upset that none of us had called her.

I finally talked to Mom a week later and she told me she was very unhappy about everything that was going on in the family. Her voice was weak but she was very defensive of Dad, saying what good care he was taking of her. I told her about the lawyer threat and she replied that he was probably concerned about everything we had said to him on Christmas night. She, of course, had been upstairs asleep and only knew whatever truly warped version of events she would have heard from him. None of this was surprising as she had spent her entire life as a wife and mother pouring oil on troubled waters. And it was all this bottling up of every injustice that was now killing her. I told her I would be over for her birthday in February.

Her birthday was on the twenty-second and none of us ever forgot it. I never remembered my father's birthday and he seldom remembered any of ours. She had made a home for all of us that was a celebration of life, a calendar of birthdays and holidays, each a cornucopia of gifts and meals that took days to prepare, while he peddled his crackpot ravings and would have no part of it. When I arrived, Mary, Finbarr and Anne were there. Mom lay on a gurney in the living room in yet another relapse. Dad was in his office downstairs and did not come up to greet me. We spent some time with her until she fell asleep and said we would be back later. I wracked my brains for some gift idea and then walking through a department store hit on the idea of an aromatherapy candle which made sense to me for someone immobilized.

The four of us walked around the woods to pass the time and talked openly about killing Dad and how unfair it was that he was not the one dying. We returned to the house with gifts and a birthday cake. One after another we went down to Dad's office to ask him to come up so we could sing Happy Birthday and with the back of his head to us he assured us he would, but the birthday candles were burning low so we sang to her without him. She liked my aromatherapy candle, a huge one with lots of wicks, but she told me later that he would never let her light it again because it was a fire hazard.

Chapter Eighteen. 1999.

Students of Finnegan's Wake do not need to be reminded that Humpty Dumpty is one of that book's basic symbols: the great cosmic egg whose fall, like the drunken fall of Finnegan, suggests the fall of Lucifer and the fall of man.

The Annotated Alice
Martin Gardner

The prospect of returning to Ireland was just the tonic our mother needed. Anne flew over that March and found a short-term rental, the home of an airline pilot who was on an assignment abroad. It was a relatively new home just outside the village of Sallins, which was itself a few miles north of the town of Naas, so they were back in the heart of County Kildare where we had all come of age. They had sold the house in Connecticut so this was indeed a one-way move for whatever time was left. The weeks rolled by and Mary went over to make plans for a fortieth birthday extravaganza for John's fortieth birthday.

Peg and I made our own plans. We crossed the Rubicon of me quitting Natsteel and they gave me a generous severance package which was to be wired from Singapore to Dublin where I would pick it up. Though Peg was now clocking up business travel and had been to Tokyo, Singapore, Mexico and Canada, she had never been to Europe. We arrived in Ireland in high spirits especially when I saw the improvement in Mom. Though she was still weak she was back to cooking and entertaining and the house in Sallins had become a revolving door of visitors. They had bought a car and while she was not yet up for driving she had Dad take her to the supermarket in Naas and accompanied him on house-hunting trips. They had now overshot the ninety-day lease agreement on the rental so this was becoming a matter of some urgency.

The day we arrived my Uncle Tony and his daughter were visiting and we joined them in the living room. When he and Dad got together they reliably put forth on all manner of opinion, generally vying with each other for the most egregious declaration. Tony, oblivious to the presence of my American girlfriend, questioned what the Americans and NATO were doing in Kosovo. Then Dad interjected to ask Peg did she know that Coca Cola had invented Santa Claus? Tony added to this that bloody Americans didn't know what to spend their money on next. Mom was not present for any of this as she was busy preparing a poached salmon dinner for all of us in the kitchen. We ate heartily and I drove a mystified Peg into Naas where we stayed at the recently converted Court House Hotel, then took off next morning for the monotonous three hour drive to Cork, punctuated only by the Rock of Cashel, Ireland's answer to the Acropolis.

We met my old friend and colleague, Dan McLoughlin, in Cork city and took a walking tour of the downtown area, culminating in one of his favourite watering holes, where we introduced Peg to the Irish delicacy, crubeens, or pigs' feet. It was the middle of summer with warm weather, blue skies and eighteen hours days which amazed Peg, but Dan and I were quick to point out to her that of course in the dead of winter this situation was reversed and we went to school in the dark and came home in the dark too. We drove on to Kinsale and stayed in a quaint hotel facing the harbour in a Georgian terrace house that had once been a bank. I showed Peg the forts and expounded on the history of the town, then Dan joined us next afternoon and we spent a glorious afternoon sitting outside The Dock Bar, looking back over the Bandon, cracking jokes, enjoying the best of times.

The following day Peg and I drove along the coast of West Cork, stopping for lunch at Bantry, where I regaled her with the significance of Bantry Bay and Napoleon and the French and then continued around the Ring of Kerry, up to Tralee and on out to Dingle where we met Billy Corr, who I explained to her was my school friend for the last two years when I went to Naas Christian Brothers, then university classmate for four years of Mechanical Engineering, apartment sharers in Schenectady while we went through GE training, and finally best man when I married Kate. He had insisted Michael should be my best man but there was already too much bad blood between us back then for that to happen. He was entirely jovial and accepting of Peg, though he also still kept up contact with Kate's family.

We returned to Naas for John's birthday bash with a day to spare so we set up a get-together with my other old friends, Bren Mick, Colman and their wives in our favourite haunt, Tommy Fletcher's. This did not go as well. For the most part they were courteous but you could tell they were ill at ease and Colman went so far as to become belligerent confronting Peg to tell her emphatically we just didn't do divorce in Ireland. This was no longer a true statement legally speaking since divorce had finally been legalized in nineteen ninety-six but he made his disapproval of this whole business abundantly clear and made Peg feel very unwelcome and relieved when they all took off back to Dublin.

Mary had certainly gone all out for this party. She had booked some place on the Newbridge Road that had a separate function room with its own bar, and a dance floor and DJ, and catered sandwiches for a hundred people. She told Peg she had done a few lines of cocaine and given John a blowjob in the toilet before it all started. Dan was invited and showed up because he knew them from the time we all went river rafting in upstate New York and he was a welcome sight for Peg after my other friends. It was a great shindig and I was also glad of Dan as I needed to mingle with old school friends who I had not seen forever and who had never left Kildare, and as the song goes were still lacking in the social graces.

We gave John a gift of a scuba mask, snorkel and fins. We had been contacted by the diving outfit on Saba to tell us they were going to do a millennium dive, where we would go down just before midnight and come up in the new century. We put the word out to everyone we knew but only John and Mary were up for it. They assured us they would get certified before the trip and we rented a house for the four of us and booked our flights. I also wanted Peg to experience a medieval banquet while we were in Ireland and Mary and John were excited to do that too. There were two possibilities, Bunratty or Dun Guaire and since the three of us had done Bunratty several times we decided to take Peg to Kinvara in Clare, stay the night, and do this smaller, more intimate version.

Kinvara is a small fishing village nestled into an inlet in the very south east of Galway Bay. The castle itself, an excellently preserved sixteenth century tower house and keep, sits on a small promontory to the north of the harbour. The Celtic Tiger economy was now in full swing and one of the beneficiaries was tourism with lots of capital going into newer bigger hotels. The Merriman Hotel was a great example of this. It is a large three story thatched building right in the middle of the village, a structure that never would have existed at the time of the architectural style it tries to depict. It would look more at home in The Bavarian Alps with its garish red windows and white walls but it was by far the best place to stay with a big cosy wood-fire heated bar, rugs and pine floors and rooms fit for Heidi.

The banquet was much more intimate than the enormous hall at Bunratty, but the entertainment was similar. There was a harpist and a couple of folk singers plus various characters dressed up as bowler-hatted leprechaun gombeen types who put on skits and the food was definitely better than what they actually ate in Ireland in the middle ages. We walked back to the village in high spirits and settled into The Thatch Bar in our hotel.

"Mary," said John as our first round arrived, "I had been meaning to tell you about this but I just didn't get around to it."

"Tell me what?" Mary asked.

"Well, you remember we were going to get tickets to Hootie and The Blowfish?"

"Yeah."

"I already had them, but you had booked your trip here, so I went anyway, with Rex."

"Okay, was it a good concert? You're more into them than me," Mary replied.

"I don't know."

"Hold on," said ever logical Peg. "you said you went?"

"We did. The place was packed. So it was a concert and I was toking up like everyone and as the band were warming up one of them came up to the mike and said that whoever was pointing that laser pointer at them had better stop."

"Those things are very dangerous," said Peg.

"So it stopped. Now I mean this place, Randall Island, was packed. I don't know how many it holds, thousands. They started on the first song and then it started again. The band stopped playing and the crowd started to get antsy. It stopped again and they started again. Hootie himself pleaded with whoever it was to stop. And then I realized it was Rex with the laser pointer! I told him to cut it out, but off he went again. Now people were starting to figure out who it was and security guards came running up to us."

"What harm was he doing?" asked Mary. "Don't lots of kids have those things?"

"Mary those things can blind you," I said.

Mary took a gulp of her Harp and cocked her eyebrows.

"the point is," said John, "he was ruining the night for everyone."

"Then why didn't you just take it off him?" Mary asked John.

"I did, in fact security confiscated it anyway. But now everyone had seen who we were and they were shouting at us, so I just couldn't sit through that for the whole show, so I grabbed Rex and we left."

"Well that was your own choice," said Mary.

"No, it wasn't. It was because Rex was being a little bollocks." John was becoming visibly worked up by Mary's defence of Rex.

"All right, all right, so are we still doing The Burren tomorrow?" I asked.

"Oh yeah, sure, Peg absolutely has to see that," said John taking the hint to change the subject.

We were planning to stay one more night so we decided that after the Burren tour we would drive around the east end of the bay to Morans Of The Weir for a feast of Galway Bay Oysters and regaled Peg with the time Tony had invited us over to the Galway Oyster Festival all those years ago. We consumed another round of drinks and were just starting on a third when Mary turned the conversation to the subject of Hancock, New York.

"I think I might just move there and ride a bike to work as a barista," she said.

"My parents used to go antique shopping there," said Peg, "but it is really off the beaten track, like in the middle of nowhere.

"Yeah, but that's the point," Mary replied, "to get away from the rat race and live the good life."

"Mary, you have just completed an advanced degree as a social worker," I reminded her, "how are you going to put that to use in a place that only has a population of a few hundred people?"

Mary pulled on her cigarette, this still being four years before there would be a total ban on smoking in any workplace, including, astonishingly at the time, pubs.

"Well, I mean why do I have to work full-time as a therapist?"

"I suppose you don't," I replied, "you're perfectly free to live the life of a derelict if that's what you want."

"Derelict!" Mary repeated. "Derelict!" Her green eyes blazed. "Who are you to call me a derelict?"

"This is the definition of dereliction," I told her, "you spent all this time and money to get yourself a great education and a career and now you are proposing to just abandon all of that."

"I'm not going to sit here and take this. John say something!"

"Well, Sean sort of has a point," John replied.

"No he bloody doesn't. I'm not going to be insulted like this. I'm going to bed."

She stood up, none too steadily, then marched out of The Thatch Bar as ramrod straight as ever her father had done in similar mood, never to set foot in the place again. The three of us stared at each other for a while then finished our drinks. This was a side of Mary that I couldn't recall ever seeing before. Usually she was the voice of reason when alcohol-fuelled shout-fests broke out, but here she was being the instigator. A pot of tea and a full Irish breakfast in the morning and this will all blow over, as it always did, I told myself, and we drained our pints and went to bed ourselves.

The phone in our room rang early next day. It was John to say they were checking out.

"Jesus, can we talk about this?" I asked.

"Nothing to do with last night in the bar," he replied.

"So Mary's calmed down?"

"We just got word that Rex has been in an accident and is in a coma. Layla got hold of Hilary who is with him now at the hospital. We're headed back to Sallins to gather our stuff and I am trying to book stand-by tickets to New York."

"Can we do anything?" I asked.

"No. We'll see how this goes and let you know about Saba."

"Yeah. Keep us in the loop."

It promised to be another warm clear day as Peg and I drove south into County Clare, through Ballyvaughan and then Lisdoonvarna, whose very pronunciation never fails to conjure up Christy Moore's immortal ballad in my head, and then on to Kilfenora to take her on a stroll through the ruined cathedral with its amazing carved crosses and headstones and then paused briefly on the bend on the road that is Killinaboy, to show her the sheila-na-gig set into the doorway of that ruined church, a rock carving of a woman pulling open her outsized vagina, variously interpreted as a pagan fertility symbol, a feminist gargoyle, and a warning that if you put your penis where it wasn't wanted it might well be bitten off. I explained that the Poulnabrone Dolmen, a giant tabletop slab supported by three vertical slabs, had once been the central chamber of a grave mound that had been washed away over thousands of years.

We ate lunch in a pub in Corofin, yet another magical place name that immediately summoned the words of the Percy French ballad immortalizing the West Clare Railway, a narrow gauge branch line that had once connected these remote and impoverished villages to the wider world. Then we criss-crossed this limestone plateau from east to west to end at the must-see Cliffs Of Moher. You could see all the way across Galway Bay to Connemara and the Twelve Bens, with the Aran Islands straddling the mouth of the belly of the dog that is the shape of Ireland. An idea formed up in my head and when we stopped back at our hotel to grab some warmer clothes before the oyster eating ritual I had them book us two tickets on Aer Arann.

This was still long before the widespread use of cellphones so we could only speculate on what was happening with Rex but, while I now had unlimited time on my hands, Peg's was very precious and the next day would be our last full day of this odyssey. We boarded the eight-seater plane at the airfield west of Galway and alighted after a short flight across the bay on the middle island of the three Aran Islands, Inis Maan. I had been to the other two islands - tiny Inisheer where I had rented bikes for Justin and Helen, with its single sandy beach facing east, protected from the ever- present Atlantic waves that pound the rocks day and night by the cliffs that rise to the west, and the far larger Inismore that supports several villages and a small network of roads.

But now, finally, I was sharing a new experience with Peg. Inis Maan was by far the least visited of these islands and a century earlier when the young playwright, John Synge, was writing down the oral tales of these people most isolated from any form of Anglican modernization he knew that he would find the best preserved folk memories here. I had read all five of his plays, his *Aran Journal*, his poems, a biography, and whatever I could find about Molly Allgood, the third and last love of his life for whom he had written his last play, *Deirdre Of The Sorrows*, before dying at the age of thirty-three. He had arrived here on a curragh from Inismore with his suitcase and fiddle and the cottage where he stayed was now preserved as a shrine to him.

Peg and I walked around the outer half of the island. taking photos with my Nikon at the blowhole and standing on the highest point where the top of the cliff juts out far beyond the base where the ocean churns relentlessly against the stone below to carve an ever deeper shelf then walked back to our starting point to settle into one of the only two pubs. Here she heard people speaking Irish for the first time and watched a hurling game on the television. Peg, unlike me, was a huge sports fan and found this fascinating. I kept wondering about the synchronicity of this Rex tragedy. Had Mary somehow sensed this? And as John told us about yet another example of this total disregard for others the previous night, I had been drawn back to his behaviour all those years ago on the trail at Yosemite. There was a pattern here but surely it was not going to cost Rex his life?

We drove back to Kildare next day and took Mom and Dad to Barberstown Castle for dinner. This was a restaurant in an old Norman tower-house that had once belonged to Eric Clapton when he lived in Ireland to dry out and dodge taxes. I had seen him in concert back then playing his huge hit, Layla, with his then girlfriend Yvonne Elliman shaking her tambourine, at the boxing stadium in Dublin. The following day Peg and I flew to London to spend a couple of nights before she flew home. We went to see the musical, *Cats*, ate great Indian food, saw the crown jewels in the Tower of London and parted company somewhat tearfully at Gatwick.

Chapter Nineteen. 1999.

West Side Story
Sondheim & Bernstein

I returned to Sallins to the news that the pilot was back and wanted to move into his own house immediately. Dad tried to involve the Garda Síochána, the Irish police, to protect this very ill woman from being evicted by this heartless creep who had turned up unexpectedly and who was being paid all the rent due to him on time. They patiently explained that they had no jurisdiction over a matter like this which would have to be decided by the courts. This sent him into a door-slamming sulk muttering about how the bastards should all be shot for refusing to come to the aid of his sick wife. The whole point of all of this was to avoid raising Mom's stress level but as usual his actions were having the opposite effect.

Then Jackie, who had long since moved back to England after Michael's meteoric disappearance, came to visit with seven year old Adam and five year old Megan. We left them at home for the first couple of days so that Dad could drive Mom and me to see the only two houses they had found that they could afford to buy for cash. The first was a bungalow a couple of miles outside Athy with moss all over the roof in an overgrown field surrounded by brambles. The second was a slight improvement with a garden wall, on the main road, if you could call it that, between Navan and Kells. Both of these were, literally, beyond The Pale. Visitors would be few and far between and it was questionable to what extent either of these locations would represent any real improvement over the loneliness of Connecticut, just less snow but more rain.

It seemed to me that if they could just pay about fifty percent more a range of much better possibilities would open up but Irish banks would not lend to people their age under any circumstances, a fact that further incensed Dad. On top of that, though the doctors on both sides of the Atlantic expected Mom to be dead by now, she was very much alive and clearly in remission, but for how long? How sensible was buying a house? I didn't have the heart to bring this up with Mom and Dad wouldn't listen to a word I said.

I walked down to The Canal Bar in Sallins that night, bought a box of Hamlets and ordered a Guinness. I had already gone to Dublin, signed a slew of confidentiality and non-compete documents, picked up my check and opened a bank account in Naas the day of John's party. What if I combined some of my money with some of theirs, bought the house for cash, then took out a mortgage on it to pay myself back? Sure, I was unemployed, but an Irish bank would have no way of knowing that, and since fifty percent of the value was there as equity they would have plenty of time to liquidate their asset should we start defaulting on the mortgage payments.

It was now eight months since she had been diagnosed. The surgery itself had almost killed her but she had recovered and it was plain as day that what kept her going was always looking forward to some brighter future. How could I not do this? But then again, how long was she going to live? Was buying a home not just the most extreme form of palliative care and should they not just rent an apartment in Dublin for the duration? On my third pint and fifth cigar I gave up on figuring this out and walked back to the house.

Next morning we all sat at the kitchen table, Dad buried in The Irish Times, Jackie coaxing the kids to eat their Rice Krispies and I ran my ideas by my mother, knowing Dad was listening.

"That's very kind of you," she said. "But if the bank refuses to lend us the money to cover your half it could be tied up for a long time."

"I'm willing to take the risk."

"Johnny, what do you think of Seán's idea?" she asked the face behind the newsprint.

"Huh? What? I wasn't listening," came the reply.

Mom carefully repeated the whole plan to him and finally he folded up the paper as he pretended to give this his most serious consideration.

"Why would we need to go to all that trouble?" he asked.

"To get a better house that isn't in the middle of nowhere," I told him.

"No, no, keep your money. We don't need any more charity from our children."

Here we go again I told myself. There was no possible response that would not slam the door permanently on all of this. I was at a loss as to how to circumvent this ever-present reverse Oedipus complex. The grapes in the hospital room had to be ridiculed because they were not his idea. The fragrant candle was beyond his comprehension. And when I had returned from London Mom and I had exchanged sly glances when I told them Peg and I had been to see the musical *Cats*. Many years earlier Kate and I had bought them a Christmas gift of a special deal I had seen in The Los Angeles Times, which was two tickets to *Cats* on Broadway with dinner at The Russian Tea Rooms included. She had loved the whole experience and he had fumed the whole time until he discovered that it was based on a book of poetry by T.S. Eliot thus legitimizing the presence of an intellectual such as himself.

They all bundled into Dad's little car to show Jackie and the kids the National Stud and The Japanese Gardens and I spent the day wandering around Naas studying the property for sale photos in the windows of the various realtors. I gathered a dozen or so flyers for houses in our price range and went over them with Mom. Armed with this she could work on Dad to not banish her to some remote culchy hellhole and remind him that she did in fact have many friends that she would like to see again in whatever time was left to her. He knew of course that I was the source of this unwelcome research and made no secret of his disdain for my interference.

And then the doorbell rang. Jackie answered it and came into the kitchen to tell Dad it was the landlord and his brother.

"Tell them there's no one here!" he barked at her.

"Dad, there are two cars in the driveway," I reminded him.

Anyway it was too late as we could now hear loud voices in the hallway. Dad bolted out of his chair and stalked out with me following him.

"You can't just come in here like this," he snarled, "this is trespassing."

"How can it be trespassing when I own the house?" asked what I now realized was pilot boy himself.

"We are legitimate tenants here and under longstanding Irish property law you can never evict us!" said Dad.

"Yes, I bloody well can," said pilot boy. "Your daughter told me she just needed a place for her parents to stay in while they sold their house in America and found one here."

"Yeah, well we're still looking," said Dad.

"And," continued the pilot, "she said it would be just the two of you whereas my neighbours have informed me that there's crowds of people coming and going all the time."

"Look, let's close the front door and come on into the living room and talk about this reasonably," I pleaded.

The brother closed the door and the four of us gathered in the front room.

"We are in fact actively house hunting," I explained. "And if you can just bear with us I would like to not have to move my mother twice."

"My wife is recuperating from a near death experience and she is under doctor's orders to rest at all times and nothing must be done that in any way would upset her," said Dad, avoiding all eye contact.

"There are only the two of them living here," I added, "but a couple of grandkids are visiting from England with their mother and I actually live in California. I'm here on business."

"Has anyone ever told you you look like George Lucas?" asked the brother.

"As a matter of fact someone asked me if I was him in a bar in London last week."

This was actually a true statement and though it was somewhat flattering to be confused with a big celebrity being told I looked like that pudgy grey-haired, plaid shirted one trick pony didn't quite hit the high note. The original Star Wars was a classic but everything else he did after that was mediocre at best, so much so that I always suspected there was a hidden hand behind that screenplay - unprepared protagonist sets off on hero quest against impossible odds, forms allies - think Hermione and Ron or Sam, Merry and Pippin, and is mentored by a sage of enormous power and wisdom - Van Helsing, Gandalf, Dumbledore - and risks his life to overcome the forces of evil intent on destroying his world. Too perfect for that buffoon to have come up with all on his own.

"How close are you to this house purchase?" asked pilot boy.

"You know we could always turn off the electricity and the water," added the brother.

"Just a minute." I strode back out to the kitchen where Mom was leafing through the house brochures with Jackie. "Found anything?' I asked.

"As a matter of fact we have," said Mom.

"This house is just down the road from where you used to live," said Jackie and handed the piece of paper to me. The price was right and it said it was walking distance to Kill village. I went back into the living room.

"We are going to put an offer on this tomorrow," I told them. "And it will be an all cash deal so should be very fast."

Pilot boy took the brochure then handed it to his brother.

"That's only a couple of miles from here," said the brother.

"Give me your phone number and I'll call you when the deal goes through," I suggested. We did that, shook hands and I walked them to the door while Dad sat in an armchair staring expressionlessly at the wall.

Mom and Mary were in daily contact about Rex who was still in a coma. He had crashed into a wall riding on a lawnmower down the hill in front of their house and was badly concussed. Hilary was my father's sister and thus my other aunt and she had been designated as emergency contact since she was the only family member within driving distance, Anne being over for the party, and Finbarr now living in Dublin with his his girlfriend, John's photographer sister, Brigid. She lived in East Hampton, an artist colony and rich people getaway at the eastern tip of Long Island. She would have had to drive all the way across Long Island into the city, then turn north over the Throg's Neck Bridge, then up the east side of the Hudson Valley. She was a huge part of my life but not of the story I am telling here. She stayed by Rex's bedside until Mary and John arrived to hear the same sordid news of the level of drugs and alcohol in his bloodstream.

Mom was now sold on the house in Kill, 96 Hartwell Green, and there was nothing Dad could do about it. Since the house hunt was now over they decided to take Jackie, Adam and Megan for a picnic in the Wicklow Mountains and I said I wanted to go into Dublin to do a few things.

"What?" queried Dad, "sure, someone will have to stay here to make sure that bastard doesn't come back and change the locks or whatever."

"He's not going to do that."

"How do you know?"

This was the man who had tweaked the phrase from *Catch 22* to say that just because you're not paranoid doesn't mean they're not out to get you. I went to bed and when I woke up next day they had already left. I made a mug of tea and searched around for the rental car keys but they were nowhere to be found. Although I now had a cellphone none of them did so there was no way to contact them. And then it dawned on me. The old batshit-crazy raving looney-tunes psychopath bollocks had either hidden the keys where it would take me all day to find them or more likely just taken them with him. I was being held hostage at Sallins against some idiotic imagined retaliation by pilot boy.

It was another glorious summer day so I walked into Sallins past yellow gorse and ripening blackberries and took up perch outside the Canal Bar. Swallows flitted overhead feasting on midges. Here there was a wider section of canal where gaudily painted restored barges and rented cabin cruisers were moored two abreast leaving room for other vessels to come and go in the main channel. I was very familiar with The Grand Canal and indeed had once tried to explain the concept of how the locks worked to my school class, but since the gormless Christian Brother in charge could not understand it himself he cut me off before I could finish my diagram on the blackboard. It is not very complicated. The Grand Canal connects Dublin with the river Shannon over a distance of about eighty miles. The high point, and therefore the source of the water, was a spring in the village of Robertstown, about ten miles west of where I now sat. From there the channels descended in both directions via a series of lock gates. If you were coming toward Robertstown from either direction you drove your barge into the lock by opening the lower lock gate, then flooded the lock to raise yourself to the next level, opened the upper gate, and continued to the next lock.

Just out of sight to my west a branch of the canal ran about two miles south to Naas ascending through five locks to end at what was called the Coal Harbour. The water was crystal clear at Robertstown but here it was already inky black as though populated by a colony of angry squid but this was actually a consequence of the peat bog that leached into it everywhere. Its principal inhabitants were majestic swans that punctuated it as ubiquitously as the ruins of castles, churches, towers and strange stone circles did the landscape everywhere. As children we learned that The Canal was a very dangerous place and we were forever being warned never to go near the edge and that the odds of surviving a fall into an empty lock were indeed dismal, but of course Dad would walk us right up to the edge and boast that he had learned to swim in The Canal.

I pictured Mary sinking through the black water in the dead of night. The Coal Harbour was a stone's throw from where she had held John's party and the tow path along the canal had no lights. I had never learned the details of what happened or who else was there and just assumed that she, Mom, and, I suppose, Dad were some combination of shocked, relieved and ashamed and just did not want to revisit the whole ordeal. Rex's self-destructive behaviour was unintentional so far as I knew, but ironically he was now the exact same age his mother had been when her young life almost came to a tragic end. I ate a couple of toasted cheese sandwiches and walked back to the house. The others were already back and Jackie was feeding Adam and Megan.

"We were wondering where you went," she told me.

"Not very far."

Jackie walked over to her handbag and fished out a set of keys.

"Sean, are these yours?" she asked. They were indeed. "I'm so sorry. I have no idea how they got into my bag."

I knew exactly how they had gotten there but it was utterly futile to bring it up.

The house purchase went very smoothly as familiar faces came into play. Old school friend John O'Reilly was the seller's agent and Dermot Fullam, long-standing family solicitor, handled the conveyancing. We took Mom for a walk-through and she immediately decided she wanted to knock out the back wall of the kitchen and put in a conservatory. It was a single-story two-bedroom bungalow but we could see that some of the neighbours had added upstairs windows and skylights and Dad decided he would do the same. My instincts were right and Bank of Ireland had no problem approving a mortgage and in due course would deposit the funds into my Irish bank account leaving my parents with a very manageable monthly payment plus enough cash for their home improvements.

We celebrated with a meal in The Dew Drop Inn, which was still the centrepiece of Kill village and considerably upgraded in both decor and fare in line with the tastes of its new ex-urban clientele. Mom was now visibly improving, her stride quickening and the musical lilt returning to her voice. Peg was always fond of the saying that everything happens for a reason and maybe she was right, but in any event I was returning to America in a far better place than I had been in since that terrible day when I had seen Mom at death's door in that hospital bed.

Chapter Twenty. 1999 - 2000.

Three Little Birds
Bob Marley

I was now well into the first draft of my next novel, which was a satirical thriller based on various anecdotes I had heard along the way at Apple and Natsteel. The story was largely set in Silicon Valley and I had high hopes that this too would result in an American deal. Apple had done a good job hushing up the decapitation of one of its employees who was trying to undo a snag in an automated handling system in Cork and there were multiple tales of memory chip heists spanning Cork to Malaysia. Peg's job was very demanding and she traveled quite a bit. However I was available to play Mister Mom so we were able to adhere to the strict fifty-fifty custody arrangement she had worked out as part of her divorce. Kelly and Charlie were with Peg every second weekend and spent two weeknights with her on weeks heading into her weekend and three weeknights on her off weekends.

Word trickled back about Rex. He came out of the coma after several days, but had a couple of weeks of manic back and forth and amnesia. He went home after about a month, and then went away to college as planned at the beginning of September. Now, the interlocutors informing us of this were a combination of Mary via Mom, Hilary, and Anne via Mom, so it was to say the least very vague. The gist of it was that Mary and John had had an enormous row about the whole thing, blaming each other, to the point where John just couldn't take it anymore, and stormed off, just like Michael, to have nothing further to do with his family.

Mary carried out her plan to move to Hancock, John sold the house, and they set about divorcing each other. We asked if they were going to do the millennium dive with us and they both assured us they were. Mary had done a scuba certification course but John had been far too busy coining money developing workarounds for his clients for the Y2K scare, whose effects were variously predicted to crash every ATM machine and navigation satellite, meaning we would resurface to global apocalypse. Bill Clinton had even set up a federal task force to avert the problem. So we gathered on Saba a couple of days early to allow John to do a crash resort course so he could do the dive.

We met at the airport on Saint Kitts to transfer to the Twin Otter plane, similar to the one we flew on to Inis Maan, which was the only passenger plane that could land and take off on what was said to be the world's shortest runway. Saba is a tiny volcanic mount with cliffs all around except for one cleft that forms the only harbour. The island has a population of about two thousand and is a part of the Netherlands. Presumably every Dutch school child learns that the peak of this volcano is the highest point in their country.

Not only is the runway tiny, it is perched hundreds of feet above the ocean. The plane routinely does a low pass to check for goats, then circles back and lands. The island has half a dozen minibus taxis and the dive shop, Sea Saba, had sent one to pick us up. He would be our driver for the duration and we would pay him at the end. There is only one road on Saba, known as The Road, and it connects the four settlements. On our first trip we had stayed at The Bottom, which is the capital, but this time we had rented a house, again through the dive shop, in the precipitous village of Windwardside. They had chosen this because there was a swimming pool adjacent to the house where they would give John his basic training. The views were spectacular and John and Mary were clearly very excited and in high spirits.

We unloaded our bags and while Peg and I were looking around they claimed the better of the two bedrooms, as the other one had two single beds that we were left to push together. There was an outdoor shower and a small living area that looked down on the village of whitewashed houses all with bright red corrugated steel roofs nestled in the emerald green foliage. Beyond lay the pristine blue Saba Marine Park with its thirty dive sites. Peg and I immediately booked a three-tank dive for the next day and told the driver to pick us up at seven a.m.

In a multi-tank dive you always do the deepest one first, so we rolled off the boat into blue depths, stabilized and then all descended together. Our destination was an underwater seamount whose peak was about one hundred and twenty feet below the surface. The rock was coral encrusted lava teeming with Black Jacks, Creole Wrasse, and Angelfish. But at this depth we were limited to fifteen minutes before starting our ascent with many safety stops. NASA uses scuba to teach weightlessness and it was easy to imagine ourselves flying over an alien world here. The second dive was the famous Diamond Rock which you can circumnavigate and as on our first visit we found moray eels hiding in the crevices and then a school of barracuda just hovering in vertical formation, staring at us, mouths agape to display their rows of sharp teeth. And on the last dive we dropped onto a sandy shoal no more than forty feet deep. A nurse shark weaved along not far off, we swam over a colony of garden eels, looking like seagrass at first until they all descended into their burrows in the sand. And the dive master beckoned and we followed him to where he had seen some Southern Stingrays almost buried in the sand and scared them up to watch them swimming gracefully away, as we had done on our previous visit, but now we were more relaxed and more observant.

Windwardside had a couple of restaurants in easy walking distance to our house. The menu was limited to how you wanted your fish of the day cooked. John was feeling good about his first day's lessons, Mary had been happy to sunbathe poolside and get in for a few dips, and we were feeling very après ocean from all the sun, saltwater and ozone.

"So Peg, who is minding your kids while you are here?" asked Mary.

"They're with my ex and his girlfriend."

"And does she have children too?"

"She has one daughter, similar age to mine."

"Does she have custody of her?"

"Not really. She spends most of her time with her father in Seattle."

"And will your husband have to give you extra days with Kelly and Charlie for having them now?"

"No," Peg replied, "because he is doing me a favour."

"What does his girlfriend do?"

"She's another engineer who was at Carnegie."

"So you went to Hancock after all?" I asked, changing the subject. Mary had never met Peg's kids so why did she want to know all this?

"Yes, I went. And yes, you were right," she replied petulantly.

"I went up there a few times, and now I know the names of the same eight people we met in the only bar every time," said John.

"I was scared to pull back the curtains," said Mary. "So I rented a condo in New London."

"Where's that and why there?" I asked.

"It's on the coast near Niantic. I wanted to be closer to Layla."

"Layla finally saw through that miserable bastard she was living with. She was getting up every day and rollerblading three miles to work. So she's living with Mary," said John.

"Rex came down for Christmas so that was nice," Mary added.

"Very nice of him to join us after getting himself thrown in the slammer his first semester," said John.

"He wasn't doing anything wrong," said Mary.

"He was under-age drinking and then he gave lip to the cop who arrested him." John turned to me. "He called me to bail him out and get him a lawyer, and when I said no he had a hissy fit and started calling me names. I hung up but he kept calling. I had to unplug the phone to make it stop."

"But he wasn't doing anything wrong," Mary persisted. "He's eighteen and he could legally drink in Ireland. A thousand dollars bail just for possession of beer! That's ridiculous."

"If he's going to break the law he should be more careful about it. Peg, did you drink in college?"

"I did and lots more. We all did but you would have to be very rowdy to get yourself arrested," Peg replied.

"Well, on the bright side it sounds like he made it through his first term of college," I interjected, "so I guess he's fully recovered from his accident."

"He's been having seizures," Mary told us.

"Yes, but they told us that was to be expected and binge drinking doesn't help," said John.

John saw Rex as responsible for his own actions whereas Mary saw her son as a victim of outside circumstances. I had used the term 'accident' to avoid antagonizing her but she was now building the case that because of his head injury he didn't exercise good judgment and fell prey to the draconian teenage drinking laws that were the product of America's puritanical heritage.

There are only two activities for tourists to Saba - diving and hiking. On our previous trip we could not hike up into the Elfin Forest, the rain forest that covers the upper reaches, because the recent hurricane had left downed trees blocking the trails, but now on this New Year's Eve, when we had to preserve both our blood nitrogen level and our sobriety for the late night dive we whiled away the afternoon wandering these heights. Then we gathered up our gear and took the taxi down to Fort Harbour to eat dinner in the restaurant above Sea Saba's shop, which was ridiculously named Restaurant Y2K. Its flamboyant gay owner, who we knew from our first trip, invited us all to party with the local islanders after the dive then provided us all with hot coffees to take on the boat.

John had concluded that he just was not ready for this dive but would come along on the boat. The sea was very choppy at the dive location, an undersea cliff that would provide an easy drift dive. Mary, Peg and I suited up along with a few other Dutch divers and the crew attached glow sticks to our buoyancy compensators and gave us each a dive light with a lanyard to attach it to our arm. We slipped into the water off the back of the boat and bobbed up and down in what was now at least a six-foot swell. The divemaster gave each of us the thumb to forefinger signal to which we all signalled back except Mary who was clearly floundering.

Even in broad daylight this would be a challenging dive entry. You would still have to get the water out of your mask, locate your BC inflator button, make sure your gauges were where you could read them and working, and tighten your weight belt. To do this in the dark on your first ocean dive in rough water was just proving too much and even Peg was holding on to me, wide-eyed. Mary was now shaking her head and the divemaster pulled her back to the boat where they undid her tank and weights and hauled her back aboard.

The rest of us descended and swam the short distance to the vertical rock face. The usual fish are of course there all the time, but here and there a lobster clung to the wall, and an octopus scuttled past us in the opposite direction in search of his dinner. This was a stressful dive, constantly looking for the other divers, using the flashlight to check and adjust our depth, and then searching for the wildlife on the wall. Moreover, it was impossible to tell what time it was, but when we got back onto the boat they popped open some champagne, poured it into plastic glasses and we all wished each other a happy new year, happy new century, and happy new millennium.

We were whisked away in the back of a pick-up truck, the four of us standing up, clinging to the roll bar, to a bar in The Bottom where hundreds of local revellers were dancing and singing and shouting above ear-splitting calypso and reggae tunes pounded out on a variety of steel drums. It was a wild night, washed down with bottles of Jamaican beer and glasses of rum and Ting, the local grapefruit soda, and I have no recollection how we got back to Windwardside but we awoke late on the first day of the twenty-first century to begin our long journeys home, Peg and I hugely satisfied with our unique accomplishment, John and Mary visibly less happy, but it was hard to tell if this was disappointment over the dive or the fact that this was as they had told us the last time they would ever be together.

Back on Saint Kitts we had all day before our flights so we took a taxi to Frigate Bay to do some snorkelling. Peg and John called it quits after a short while, but Mary and I kept going, perhaps reminded of much earlier good times on the Costa Del Sol. We eventually swam back, towelled off, and took a taxi back to the airport. Peg kept staring at me, tightlipped, then walked on quickly ahead of me into the terminal. Something was clearly up, but it was only when we planted ourselves in the duty-free while Mary and John sorted out some details about their flights that she told me what it was.

"While you were swimming with Mary, John told me that you left Kate because she got sick and that you'll do the same to me."

This was a bolt from the blue. It was like that old adage - when did you stop beating your wife? Where had this come from? John was clearly trying to drive a wedge between Peg and me. Was this his way of coming onto her? After all he himself was now officially single again. And Peg's radiant beauty was now on full display in her shorts, tank top and sunglasses. She was a brilliant, wickedly funny person whose smile with those two rows of perfect pearly white teeth literally lit up the room. What a bastard. I fumed away in silence for a while, shaking my head. Peg, like most Americans, took people at their word. I, like most Irish, looked for the hidden meaning.

Maybe John wasn't hitting on her and was just jealous of me, but either way it was pretty despicable. At first I considered confronting him then and there about it but that would just amplify the whole thing and God only knew what zany interpretation of it Mary would come up with. I assured Peg as best I could that that was not what had happened and that Kate had

had health issues for over half the two decades plus we had been together so John's argument made no logical sense. I didn't want this trip to end on a bad note so we walked around the jewelry stores until we found a pair of pearl earrings that Peg liked and I bought them for her.

Mary later attributed Peg's sulky behaviour to the fact that I had bought her earrings instead of an engagement ring, a typical wrong conclusion from her and a harbinger of many more that would follow. First, we were still undecided about getting married. Sure, we were over the rebound fears, and she was gently pressing me for a decision, but we were not there yet, and besides, who would be stupid enough to buy such an important symbolic object in a duty-free gift shop on a tiny island in the Caribbean. Pearls, yes, this was the place and what you saw was what you got. But a fucking diamond ring?

John, by all accounts, had decided to leave his two problem children for Mary to sort out. That might well be because he had had enough of her namby-pamby psychobabble and refusal to hold them accountable for their atrocious actions but in any event he was now out of the picture as far as my family was concerned. I never needed to see, hear from, or talk to him again. I wanted to dash across the departure lounge and beat the shit out of him. Instead we waved goodbye, boarding cards in hand and I vowed never to have anything to do with the bastard again.

Good riddance and to hell with him and the horse he rode in on.

Chapter Twenty-One. 2000 - 2002.

Soak Up The Sun
Sheryl Crow

By the summer of Two Thousand when I again returned to Ireland the alterations to the house in Kill were mostly complete. Mom had her conservatory, now overflowing with house plants and wicker furniture. She was also doing some real gardening, planting flowers and bushes in the back garden with the help of her oldest surviving friend, Carmel. Mary had once speculated that Carmel was Ena's Lesbian lover but no evidence has ever surfaced to support yet another of my sister's inane theories. There was never a man in Carmel's life and my suspicion was that Dad saw her as a legitimate target along the way, but a woman that scrubbed the floors of churches to better purify herself was probably a long shot.

The previous year, Jack Van Zandt, my American publisher, had handed me an advance copy of a book that his company, Roberts-Rinehart, were about to publish. It was called *The Committee,* by Sean McPhelimy, a British TV documentary producer. The title referred to the ULCCC - the Ulster Loyalist Central Co-ordinating Committee - a shadowy organization comprising politicians, police officers, paramilitaries and other stalwarts. Note that the word "Unionist" is not used. What this gang of extremists wanted was an independent Ulster, run by these so-called loyalists, whose ultimate aim was to ethnically cleanse the province of Catholic nationalists by whatever means necessary. Their stock in trade was the planning, execution and cover-up of political assassinations.

I now had enough reviews, press-cuttings and interviews to be confident in my ability as a prose writer so I had turned my attention to screenwriting. This was not as easy as I had at first thought but when I finally read the HBO script for *The Hungry Earth* I found that it bore no resemblance to the novel and was further motivated to try my hand at this. I eventually taught myself the Hollywood page-a-minute format and cranked out a ninety minute movie idea which had no hope of ever being made. *The Committee* was a much better opportunity and one of the reasons for my trip this summer was to meet up with Sean McPhilemy in Oxford.

The Committee was a book about a documentary about a conspiracy. When it first aired it caused consternation and immediately led to litigation against all involved. It brought McPhilemy's successful career to a crashing end and after a good meeting in which he endorsed my proposed adaptation he paused, as he was driving me back to the station, outside what had been his home in better days, and burst into tears. He told me he was now treated like Kryptonite by everyone. Worse was to follow and while we had no problem finding an agent to shop my screenplay around the same curse now haunted this too. A couple of well-heeled car dealers named in the book filed a hundred-million dollar lawsuit against both McPhilemy and Roberts-Rinehart. The plaintiffs eventually settled out of court for a million dollars after spending two million of their own money but it was the end of Roberts-Rinehart, my US publishers.

I walked down to the village one morning to buy black pudding, white pudding, rashers, sausages, eggs and tomatoes for Mom, Dad, Anne and myself and began cooking this on the flimsy bockety pan that I found below the cooker. I was constantly having to move the food around to avoid having the rashers burned at one end and raw at the other and after breakfast I drove into Naas to the old hardware shop still thriving on Main Street next door to Kavanagh's, yet another venerable watering hole from my schooldays. I bought a heavy cast iron frying pan and when I got back to the house I found Mom on her own attending to her house plants. I explained my gift and put the kettle on. We sat at the kitchen table for a while chatting and the conversation turned to the subject of Peg.

"I have to say I am very surprised," said my mother, "at you taking up with a woman who abandoned her own children."

I was flabbergasted. "What are you talking about?"

"I was told she just walked out on her husband and children."

I wanted to yell out: "who told you that?" But there was no point and no need. It was my bitch sister of course. Even though I had been her staunchest ally always and even though I was the only family member who had been unambiguous about her sexual abuse claims she still felt this overwhelming need to run me down in the eyes of my mother. In all families we unwittingly assume roles and in ours I was the hero, Michael was the scapegoat, Mary was the princess, Finbarr was the lost child and Anne was the baby. I was not the hero by choice, I had been assigned this role by my mother, tasked with setting an example for my younger siblings to follow, but the road to my hell was paved with my mother's good intentions.

Why did Mary not reciprocate my support for her? Wasn't my fall from grace by my now well-known fling with Geraldine and my far bigger sin of leaving Kate enough? No, now my new lover had to be laid low too so as to magnify my corruption. Mary knew that for Mom her children were her world. She knew that telling her that Peg had left hers was one of the worst things she could say about Peg and by extension about me for wanting to be with such an awful person. Moreover she knew this was not true and that had been reaffirmed on Saba. And all of this fed into her own feminist martyr narrative of having to deal with what she now contended was her brain-damaged son as well as full custody of her troubled teenage daughter.

Patiently, I went over the situation one on one with my mother about Peg and her children. At no time had she ever left them. Because she was the one who wanted to end the marriage and because she had no grounds for telling her husband to leave their home it fell to her to find her own place to live which she quickly did in very close proximity. To conflate moving out of her husband's house with abandonment of her kids was a stunning insult to Peg, and Mary well knew it. Peg lived for Kelly and Charlie and though Mom would not live to see the outcome, as a mother Peg would leave Mary in the dust.

Mom was genuinely relieved to hear my version of this. She wanted to see the best in people. She wanted us all to be happy. She repeated over and over that she never wanted to leave the house we lived in for the first ten years of her marriage, so much so that I had driven by it lately and struggled to see what appeal this truly wretched little semi-detached unheated concrete cube with its tiny front and back patches of ground surrounded by waist-high block walls could possibly have for her. But I was missing the point. The building was just shelter from the elements, and what she missed was the people, the neighbours with children our ages, the village shops that she could walk to, the bus that took you any time of day into the centre of Dublin along the Liffey quays, the proximity to where she herself had grown up, that home where all's accustomed ceremony.

The house she was living in now was the best approximation possible of all of this and was a fusion of that early home and the later homes in Cabinteely and at the other end of Kill village. Everyone she knew had by now been here to visit her and the very fact that they all knew she was here and that they were welcome any time sustained and indeed healed her. I took enormous pleasure in this outcome, certain that it was prolonging her life, and that she was finally immersed one last time in that old familiar Irish world that had provided her with so much happiness over the years.

I returned to California but not before being castigated, belittled, verbally horsewhipped and ridiculed for the cast iron skillet which any moron could see was far too heavy for an infirm woman to lift and was hence a serious danger in the kitchen, all this from a man who could not and never had boiled an egg in his life. Peg was predictably apoplectic when I told her what Mary had said about her and whatever misgivings she had had about my sister up till now this was a rift beyond any possibility of repair.

On November twenty-first Peg and I were married on the Hawaiian island of Kauai. It was a simple ceremony officiated by a minister who blew into a conch shell and attended by the couple who had rented us their condo on Poipu Beach and a turtle watching from below the windy bluff. Peg wore a sleeveless white cotton dress with her hair in a rare updo and I wore khaki shorts and a purple Hawaiian silk shirt which I later discovered was the uniform of the wait staff in the Hyatt Hotel next door. We dined on the lanai of a sugar plantation mansion and scuba-dived on lava tubes teeming with sea life. There were clown fish darting in and out of huge sea anemones, cleaner shrimp on the backs of turtles and an amazing variety of moray eels.

We ate tuna poke between dives, then took a helicopter ride around the island, hovering halfway down the spectacular four-hundred-foot Manawaiopuna Falls, better known as Jurassic Park Falls, then next day took a movie tour in a minibus to see King Kong mountain, the horse trail from Elvis' Blue Hawaii, and the landscape where we first see the dinosaurs in Jurassic Park. We kayaked into Wailua Falls and ate lunch at Hanalei Bay.

There were feral chickens everywhere, a legacy from some long forgotten hurricane that had destroyed every poultry shed. We had a stopover on Oahu on the way back and dived off Waikiki Beach onto an old fighter plane that had run out of fuel and was now a reef housing shoals of squirrel fish, then visited Pearl Harbour and saw the oil still oozing up from the USS Arizona, grave to over a thousand sailors, then danced the night away at some nightclub where Peg would flash her tits at me now and again to be sure of my full attention.

Wolfhound Press now had the manuscript for my Silicon Valley novel. I had given it the working title *D-RAM* since the plot centres on the theft of memory chips and was to some extent based on true events. The folks at 68 Mountjoy Square were perplexed as to why I would want to name the book after a measure of Scotch whisky. In the end we settled on *The Memory Trap* as the title, which did in fact speak to many of the story's elements. I wanted to get this novel out while the news spotlight was still on Silicon Valley with the ongoing dot-com revolution but there was no way to expedite the annual rhythm of their publishing calendar. To make matters worse HBO, who had now converted the movie screenplay into a mini-series, had shelved *The Hungry Earth* altogether. Once known for a steady output of quirky movies they now had far greater ambitions. They were going to throw their entire original programming budget at an adaptation of the Stephen Ambrose book, *Band Of Brothers,* an account of the exploits of Easy Company of the Hundred and First Airborne during World War Two, pitched to them by Tom Hanks and Steven Spielberg. And after that came Game Of Thrones.

Early the next year on one of Peg's non-kid weekends we drove up to Sonoma in her new silver BMW to stay at a B&B that had been recommended to us just outside Guerneville, a decidedly rainbow community near the mouth of The Russian River. We spent the afternoon wine-tasting, mostly Pinot Noir, before arriving at the Ridenhour House, which we renamed The Ridden Whore for our own amusement. This was right next to Korbel, America's best known brand of fizz, which stayed open later on Saturdays so we decided to do a last tasting here. And of course, as invariably happens at the last winery of the day, they had no problem persuading us to sign up to their club in order to waive the tasting fee, buy a few bottles at the member discount, and rest assured that we could cancel at any time. We frolicked in the outdoor hot tub later, steam rising up to the pine trees and the stars, sipping our bubbly bounty before slipping under the down comforter on our antique bed.

The breakfast of home-made muffins and salmon and spinach quiche was every bit as good as our friends had promised. We set out west through Guerneville to the coast at Jenner and turned south toward Bodega Bay. Sheryl Crow blared from the speakers until the last song on the album played and the music stopped. The CD changer in the Beemer was in the back and we had not set it up to play anything else so we drove on in silence with the rocks and sand and surf on our right until Peg, out of nowhere said:

"Would you let your teenage daughter stay with the man who molested your sister?"

This was all a bit cryptic. "I'm sorry, stay where? With who?"

"I'm talking about Mary sending Layla to stay with your father."

This had happened over a year earlier.

"They were trying to get her away from her drug dealer boyfriend," I said.

"But why there of all places?"

"I don't know the answer to that, maybe there was no other choice."

"Would you send Helen to live with someone you knew for a fact was a pedophile rapist?' Peg persisted.

"Of course I wouldn't do that."

"Of course," Peg repeated. "So I just don't think your father molested Mary."

"You think she's making it up?" I asked incredulously.

"Well, we know she makes things up when it suits her." Peg was clearly going back to what Mary told Mom about her. I tensed up so much that I almost swerved into an oncoming car. I nosed into a sand dune and jammed on the brakes.

"Look, just because Mary is a certifiable nut job doesn't mean it didn't happen, in fact that might be the very reason she's so mentally and emotionally unstable."

"I don't believe her. Your father is a lot of things but he's not that."

Peg was an excellent judge of character and also very logical. After her first trip to Ireland she had researched the relationship between Coca Cola and Santa Claus and e-mailed Dad what she had found and after the very first meeting in the hospital when he had declared that all American women were cute hoors it had taken me forever to persuade her that he was not calling her a hooker. But she was flat-out wrong here and my bile was rising.

"You didn't know Mary before any of this came out," I yelled. "She was a useless, depressed layabout who never had a job, dressed herself and her children in rags, left them to fend for themselves every morning, and smoked and drank herself to sleep in the small hours every night. This complete turnaround that she has made is what's hard to believe, but there it is. She has two degrees, a steady job, in fact a career!" Now I was really losing it. "How do you explain that?" I glared angrily at my silent wife. "You can't unless this actually happened. Look, I hate even thinking about it. It has poisoned all of us, but what other explanation is there?"

Peg stared out the window at the surf. A flock of pelicans skimmed over the waves in the opposite direction. We sat there in silence for a long time until I got out and reloaded the CD player, and then we drove around Bodega Bay lost in our own thoughts, evading any further discussion on the long drive home.

Chapter Twenty-Two. 2002 - 2003.

Poor Desdemon, I am glad thy father's dead.
Thy match was mortal to him, and pure grief
Shore his old head in twain. Did he live now
That sight would make him do a desperate turn,

Graziano
Othello, Act V, Scene 2, lines 211-214
William Shakespeare

There was nothing I could do to accelerate the publication of *The Memory Trap* so I turned my attention to yet another project. My original and still unpublished book was born out of a love of all things Irish. While everyone consumed the endless regurgitations of King Arthur and Robin Hood almost no one other than a handful of nerdy Irish school-children such as myself were even aware that Ireland had its own rich mythology. And then there was Shakespeare and the English Renaissance and the gormless adoration of all things Elizabethan, from her virginity to her humiliation of the hapless Spanish Armada. There was another side to this story that was all but ignored, and I wanted to set that straight.

Apple had come out with a piece of software called Final Cut Pro which allowed just about anyone to create a professional documentary on a desktop Macintosh. It even had a feature you could click on called the Ken Burns Effect after the famous documentarian which allowed you to set a beginning and end point that was as if you were panning the camera across an image. I wanted to tell the story of the Elizabethan conquest of Ireland from the Irish side and expose the self-serving greedy racist bigotry that was behind it. I arrived in Ireland in the summer of two-thousand and one armed with a HD video camera and copies of *The Twilight Lords*, O'Faoláin's *The Great O'Neill* and Friel's *Making History* to shoot whatever coverage was to be had of the war that culminated in the Battle of Kinsale, 1601.

When I arrived at my parents' house I found both of Mary's kids living there. Layla was commuting to a job in Dublin as a receptionist at an architectural firm while Rex idled away his days either smoking pot in Naas with his uncle David, John's brother, or boozing in the Dew Drop Inn.

161

Mom and Dad showered glowing praise on their granddaughter, the up-and-coming architect, while Dad muttered incessantly about Rex passing out on the couch every night and then urinating on it in his sleep. Mary was nowhere to be seen. She had sold her house and relocated her children to Ireland, where they could drink alcohol legally and get free higher education while she spent her divorce winnings on a months-long trip around the world.

Finbarr was still living in Dublin with Brigid and was between jobs, so he was happy to drive me around the various locations that would feature in my documentary. We started in Armagh where Hugh O'Neill had lived as the Earl of Tyrone and ruled the eastern part of Ulster. There was not much left of what had once been the most modern palace in sixteenth century Ireland. The foundations and the first few feet of the brick walls were all that remained and even those were inside a compound of army and police radio transmitters. O'Neill had been sent to England as a youth to learn their more civilized ways and he had returned filled with the best ideas of the time. He ruled as a Gaelic chieftain but sided with the English when it suited him. He is even said to have taken part in the massacre of an earlier Spanish expedition which was besieged in a promontory fort at their landing point at Smerwick Harbour on the Dingle peninsula, and didn't spare any of the local girls they found there either. Armagh Cathedral, with its stained glass windows, provided better visuals, as did driving further south to the ruins of Mellifont Abbey, the church and convent where O'Neill finally surrendered, unaware that Queen Elizabeth was already dead. Finbarr was an even more avid reader and history enthusiast than me and we made the most of the long days to amass many hours of coverage. I eventually took the project to the BBC but they were not very interested and cited other examples that had not been well-received and told me they had concluded that people were simply not interested in other people's history.

Returning to Kildare we all took Mom to the symphony at Earlsfort Terrace, the site of my first-year engineering lectures before being converted to the National Concert Hall. Mom was now seventy-two and so far as I could tell she was as fit and healthy as any of us could expect to be at her age. She had emigrated to America at the age of fifty-two and promptly taken up skiing, no small achievement as I knew from my own attempts at snowboarding. A few months earlier she and Dad had flown to South Africa to visit Michael and gone on a safari and come back with great tales of sightings of elephants and rhinos and Michael being charged by a hippo. It was now coming up on three years since her diagnosis, a truly miraculous outcome. But if I was to attribute this to Mom's newfound happiness, then I could hardly avoid my longstanding conclusion that Ena's opposite outcome had been provoked by her unhappiness. She died of shame while her sister lived on and on in innocence.

I returned to Morgan Hill with a wedding present of two Waterford Crystal champagne flutes that Mom had thoughtfully bought and kept for us after a conversation about our wine-tasting enthusiasm. Peg was still appalled at what Mary had done and when Mary on her return leg of her world tour landed on our doorstep it didn't take a whole lot of wine before Peg, for whom the expression to-suffer-in-silence was absent from her lexicon, lit into her about everything. How could she leave her incontinent layabout pot-smoking son to be a burden on his terminally ill grandmother? And what mother would leave their teenage daughter to stay with the man she had publicly accused of father-daughter incest? I wanted to crawl under the dining-room table and disappear. Mary hemmed and hawed, never answering directly, complained about jet-lag, and eventually slithered off to bed.

Then, within a few months, increasingly alarming news reached us of Mom having bouts of weakness, being bedridden, and even asking to be taken to the hospice at Harold's Cross in Dublin, not far from where she had grown up, to just be taken care of and try to recuperate. None of the denizens of the house in Kill were in the slightest way nurturing toward her. Dad mechanically doled out her medications but absolutely refused to engage on any level with her approaching mortality. Mary's kids were no more than a pair of nincompoops deposited there by their self-absorbed mother and Finbarr, by far the most empathetic person within reach, had split with Brigid and now lived in a rented house underneath the West Link bridge where he was employed as a resident engineer, an hour's drive away in Dublin.

In the new year it became clear that she was now in an irreversible decline and we all made plans to get to Ireland. On the flight over, always a night flight such that I would usually watch movies and drink wine, I did neither. Instead, I worked on a eulogy on my laptop until the battery died then dozed for the duration. Finbarr picked me up, and we drove straight to the hospice. Mom was in bed on a morphine drip, Dad sitting next to her on one side and Anne on the other. She was asleep when I came into the room but she woke up and smiled. Her face had gone from wrinkled to crumpled but because she had refused any more chemotherapy her hair was intact. In a rare display of affection Dad rubbed her cheek with the back of his hand. She had told me on all of my visits how well he was taking care of her but I could never be sure if this was really true or a continuation of her lifelong project to smooth over the ever present tensions born of the bad memories of a lifetime that might erupt like some dormant volcano at any time.

Dad asked about my flight and seemed genuinely glad to see me. I told Mom that Justin and Helen sent their best wishes and filled in the time telling them all about Justin, who had graduated high school the previous June, moving up to Tahoe to live with some friends, trading in his surfboard for a snowboard, and working the slopes as a lifty, and about Helen who now had her driver's license and was ever the socialite. She had landed her first job serving pizza by the slice at Pizza My Heart in downtown Santa Cruz. The perks of this job included free CDs from the Virgin record store next door and free entry to any movie at the local cineplex in exchange for contraband free pizza. She had another year of school to go, but had been badly bullied, such that we had to have her privately tutored for a while, then got her into another school district that eschewed the noble idea of bussing in the Mexican agricultural worker kids from the farms further around the bay.

Mom and Dad had been to see us at our first beach house, so they knew the area, and knew what a beautiful place my kids were growing up in. I reminded them of some of the things we had done, the beaches, the piers at Aptos and Capitola and Santa Cruz and the hike we took in the redwoods. Of course, like just about everyone, they had fallen in love with Carmel By The Sea, strolling around the cafes and art galleries. Mom drifted off to sleep and Finbarr and I left. Outside the room we were met by two ladies who already knew Finbarr. Their actual profession was unclear but what they were intent on communicating to us was that there was not much time left and that while they could control the pain the morphine might stop Mom's heart before the cancer itself ran its course.

We took turns at the overnight vigil and next morning Finbarr went to get Mary, and then Michael and Janet, from the airport. Michael got into a heated argument in customs over whether the case of wine he had brought from South Africa was subject to duty. He argued that it was all wine from his personal collection and they conferred with each other as to what the law was about bringing wine into the European Union. Eventually when he told them what he had paid for it they all laughed and told him to just go on. Even in the finest restaurants in South Africa, as I would later learn, twenty dollars is the most you can expect to pay for a great bottle.

That night we were all sitting around the bed watching Mom sleep when she suddenly sat bolt upright and stared around wild-eyed.

"Where am I?" she asked. Then she noticed me. "Sean, get me out of here! I don't want to be here. Take me away from here!" I started to speak, but she had already slumped back down, so I hurried out to find the same two women as before. I told them what had happened and one of them nodded.

"This happens near the end but we can control it."

I borrowed Finbarr's car and drove Michael and Janet back to his house. They were exhausted. I told them to have a shower and lie down and I would stay by the phone. Two hours later the dreaded call arrived. I told Michael and asked if he wanted to go in with me. He seemed to be half asleep and said no to just go ahead. I cried the whole way to the hospice and found the others in tears too, with Finbarr lying across Mom, sobbing uncontrollably. Dad sat on the far side of the bed, holding her hand, as forlorn as I have ever seen him.

Time stopped. My mind was flooded with the memory of who she had been. I had not known her father because he died of cancer when I was three, but I had all of his love letters to Granny, dating back to nineteen-twenty and I knew of his goodness through reading them over and over. Granny had lived on to die just a couple of years before Ena. She lived on and off with us and was forever ironing and folding my clothes. Mom had the kindest, gentlest parents in the world, a railway clerk and a seamstress who never owned more than a bicycle and a sewing machine. His passion was fly fishing and hers was romance novels and other than that they devoted themselves to raising their two daughters to be devout Catholics as they were themselves. The older one had succumbed to temptation and perished, but now here lay the perfect product of that union, surrendering to death a month shy of her seventy-second birthday.

Everyone whose life was touched by my mother was the better for it. We all, though we might not know it, became a part of her Apollonian world, a place of light and goodness and generosity. I grew up watching her buy ice cream after Sunday mass and bake Christmas cakes and plan turkey and stuffing and make my friends and girlfriends welcome any time in our home. There was an aura, some intangible presence, about her that made you strive to be better than you were because you knew you were loved and should love back in return. From when I was a small child MotherKenny and Auntie Nell always told me my mother was a saint and here she now lay without a furrow on her brow, as chaste a woman as had ever walked this Holy Ground.

Finbarr composed himself and Dad let out a long sigh.

"Sean, I'm just exhausted from all of this," he said, then stared across at me and continued, "you'll have to take over from here and do everything."

I nodded and then began to wonder what that meant. Mom had told me over the last couple of years that while she was afraid of pain she was not afraid to die but that any time she brought the subject up he would vehemently hush her as though the very mention of the word might bring it on or, more likely in his convoluted thimble, that like some latter-day King Canute, not acknowledging this inevitability would hold it at bay forever.

The most recent funeral I had been to had been my aunt Hilary's husband Liam's, five years earlier. He died of prostate cancer which had it been detected sooner was entirely treatable. He knew he was dying, Hilary knew he was dying, his family and all the rest of us knew it. There was fear in his eyes those last few weeks, but they installed him in a bed in the living room and brought Uncle Michael, Dad's and Hilary's brother, over to be his constant companion though because of the oxygen set-up Michael had to chain-smoke his cigarettes outside in the bitter Long Island cold. Everything had been meticulously organized, from the flowers and the coffin, to my cousin Brian's eulogy, to the type of coffin, and the exact location and orientation of the grave plot, such that he would be buried facing east toward Ireland forever.

Nothing had been done here by anyone. There was no grave plot, nor even a decision on which cemetery. No-one had alerted her local parish church nor engaged an undertaker and since none of that was yet known it was impossible to book a venue for the tea and sandwiches for the mourners after the burial. It was as if she had just been hit by a bus, crossing the road. That kind of thing did actually happen I told myself, so there must be some mechanism for organizing a funeral in the event of sudden death. Thankfully her oldest friend, Carmel O'Donoghue, an expert on all matters ecclesiastical, had been giving this some thought and she now began to make phone calls and come up with suggestions.

The next day we bought a simple pine coffin because Dad was adamant that Mom would not want to waste a lot of money on something that was just going to be buried in the ground anyway. It was delivered to the hospice chapel, the girls selected what they thought was her favourite outfit, and the staff moved her body and dressed her. Word of her demise was now spreading rapidly and we had a viewing that evening that attracted some friends living in Dublin city. Those of us staying with Finbarr drove under the massive flyover bridge he was building upriver along the old road to the Strawberry Beds for a few pints in The Wren's Nest, and I went over my eulogy with them.

Finding both a priest and a church was very time-consuming. Her local parish simply had no priest available that week. Walkinstown, where she had been baptized, seemed like the next logical choice, but there was some complication there with parking spaces. We moved on to Clondalkin parish church, where Mom and Dad where we had all been baptized, and they acquiesced. Next day Peg and Kevin flew in and we had the removal service from the hospice to the church and more people showed up for those prayers. After that we all gathered at Dad's house and one more time I read out my proposed eulogy. I got a couple of suggestions, which I included. Then I offered to have someone else read it out on the day, or even make up something of their own, but there were no takers. Michael said he would think about it.

The morning of the funeral, day three of these proceedings, it rained incessantly, and a gale drove the icy drops onto our faces such that umbrellas were useless. The church was as full as it ever was for a Sunday mass and

I delivered my eulogy and told everyone that we would be serving food at The Green Isle Hotel, a well-known landmark on the Naas Road not far away. Mary, Anne and Layla bawled throughout the Mass, their hair unbrushed, their clothes unkempt, in true banshee fashion. The cemetery we had decided on was also very close, Newlands Cross, and we all agreed that this laid her to rest at an intersection of the three places she had lived in Ireland for most of her life. We shivered and huddled in the bitter rain as they lowered her into the open grave and then traipsed gloomily back to our cars.

Peg and I now had a room at The Cill Dara Hotel around the corner from Dad's house. The whole family was going to gather around the kitchen table for a meal that night, which Kevin and Peg were planning and preparing. There would be eleven of us and it was going to be a tight squeeze. Peg suggested we should just make one big salad but Mary was having none of this. We were going to do the salad as a separate starter course. Period. End of discussion. Michael had set up his video in the living room and was showing us a movie of elephants and other wildlife in South Africa. The main sound was of his own smoker's cough, and when I told him I didn't know elephants coughed it just went over his head.

We gathered around the table and suffered through Mary's salad idea, which meant clearing all those plates away to serve the main course. I was now the one that was exhausted. I had given everyone something to do just to keep them busy, but I had borne the brunt of the funeral arranging. Mary, who had told Peg she just wanted to sit back and observe it all even went so far as to tell me and the whole table that they could have pulled it off without my help such was the scorn she felt compelled to heap on her ever loyal oldest brother.

"Here, Sean, try some of this wine," said Michael. "This is unique to South Africa. It's the only place where Pinotage grapes are grown." He poured wine for everyone, then started uncorking another bottle. "In fact, we've been making wine way longer than California. Goes back to when the Portuguese first arrived. Might be even older than most French wine."

"I'm not sure about that math," I replied.

"How do you know?" he asked a bit more snarkily.

"Let's see, the papal schism was in the twelfth century, right Finbarr?"

"I think so," Finbarr replied.

"And they brought the grapes with them to make what we now call Chateau Neuf Du Pape meaning new palace of the pope."

"Yeah, that's right," said Finbarr, the family's most prominent historical authority.

"But you don't know when they actually started making wine," Michael chided, "and we do know there are four hundred year old wineries in Stellenbosch."

"Fine," said I, "but we do know there were actual wine bars in Pompeii which were buried in lava and ash when Mount Vesuvius erupted back in what? The first century?"

"I was talking about France, not Italy," Michael retorted, decidedly testy now.

"And then there's Greece," I added. "They had a god of wine..."

"Bacchus," said Finbarr.

This was too much for Michael. "You hijacked my mother's funeral!" he yelled across the table.

"I did what?"

"I wanted to say something in the church!"

"Then why didn't you?"

"Because you wouldn't let me."

"It was mentioned last night," added Janet, referencing my offer to have someone else read the eulogy I had written.

"I didn't stop you," I replied, genuinely non-plussed by this outburst.

"Yes, you did. I had made notes and I had them in my pocket and, when I signalled to you, you ignored me."

"I didn't see you. Why didn't you stand up?"

"Because it was too late. As soon as you stopped talking everyone started clapping and you just walked back to your seat. I really fucking hate you and if I was on the other side of this table I would stab you to death with this knife." He brandished one of Mom's old fake-ivory-handled steak knives.

Peg jumped to her feet, knocking her chair over. "Sean, I'm leaving. Take me back to the hotel!"

I looked around but no-one made eye contact with me or attempted to intervene. I stood up and walked out after Peg and so ended the three days of commemoration of Mom's death.

Chapter Twenty-Three. 2003 - 2013.

◇ *This is the last call for Ellis island,*

These are the last words

I'm ever going to hear you say... ◇

Mary Black

Seamus Cashman emailed to say he was ill and then a while later I was blind-copied on an email that presumably went to all of his authors to tell us he had sold Wolfhound Press to a company called Merlin Media. They told me they hoped to publish *The Memory Trap* in two-thousand and three. This further delay bothered me enormously because the story line was based on technology that kept evolving and it was quickly becoming a Clinton Era period piece. I tried my hand at another feature film screenplay, a biopic about the playwright John Millington Synge and duly sent this off to The Irish Film Board. Mary's kids moved back to America and Finbarr moved in with Dad and started paying him rent.

Helen graduated high school that summer and bolted for Lake Tahoe to live with Justin. The male to female ratio at a winter sports resort was about ten to one and Helen took full advantage of this. She worked as a waitress until the season started and then landed a job in the lost and found office at Heavenly. This was a cushy indoor job that came with the added perk of an endless supply of free hats, goggles, gloves, sunglasses and scarves. Justin lasted one more season but tired of the same potheads and moved to San Francisco, where, instead of smoking pot, he became adept at growing pot indoors in his Sunset apartment, walking distance to excellent surfing. Cannabis was still not legal for recreational use but it was for medical use and there was a whole industry of doctors who would give you a card for just about any pretext. Justin got top dollar for his crops as he grew strains that had very high THC content.

In the spring of two-thousand and three I came back to Ireland for the long-delayed publication Tof my novel. They did a good job, getting me onto morning TV on the new Channel Three, a few radio slots, and a two-page spread in one of the Sunday tabloids, basically a then and now piece about

Kate and I, for which I had Helen dig out an old photo taken in a photo booth in London, me with my mullet and Kate in a French beret. I had hoped this book would get me a US deal, but it didn't. Merlin did however sell a Russian translation, so I guess I was a hit on the Moscow subway for a while. Dad drove me around and was proud of keeping all thirty of Mom's house plants alive. I borrowed the car one day to visit the grave and was saddened though not surprised to see that he had done nothing about a headstone. There she lay under the tiny wooden marker that we had been given free while all around her shiny granite and marble slabs stood in long lines proudly announcing the names of the loved ones lying below.

Merlin also told me on that trip that they did not intend to publish any more fiction but what they didn't add was that neither did they intend to pay any further royalties on the titles they were still selling. And then I got my hands on The Irish Film Board reader report on my script. By now I had been in the writing game for long enough to have accumulated many, many rejections, but this one was in a league of its own. Whoever this reader bitch was she had concluded that if you took the famous names out of this - Yeats, Joyce, Maud Gonne, Lady Gregory, Synge himself - there was nothing there. But this was just arrant nonsense. It handily covered Synge's artistic life from his first visit to The Aran Islands, to the genesis of his plays, to The Playboy riots, and his three romantic relationships, culminating in his tragic death at the age of thirty-three.

It was as if no-one who was not Neil Jordan or Jim Sheridan should dare darken their door. Perhaps by now that syphilitic sheila-na-gig has died a long, slow, excruciatingly painful death and finds herself right at the centre of the ninth circle of Dante's inferno, her eyelids held open by Lucifer himself, her tits forever gnawed on by the starving Count Ugolino and his sons and grandsons, forced to read aloud over and over the first effort of the worst film school students of all time, wearing only a rusty barbed wire thong too small for her fat arse that is wired to a Van De Graaf generator that shocks her to a frazzle if ever she pauses. Am I being a bit too unkind here?

That next season Helen was hired by Kirkwood, a ski resort that trained would-be Olympians. By now she was a very fast snow-boarder with offers of sponsorship, but that would mean traveling all over the USA which did not appeal to her, so she advanced to the position of race-timer, learning to operate very precise timing equipment. When the winter season at Tahoe ended she was asked to accompany the timing gear to a sister resort in New Zealand, Treble Cone. She made lots of new friends there, as she always does, and had her boyfriend join her at the end of the season to tour the waterfalls and the The *Lord Of The Rings* shooting locations and sets.

Justin was now putting himself through college at San Francisco State, living off his cannabis crop, and would go on to earn a degree in business and nutrition. He would use his EMT qualification to work the Burning Man and Reggae On The River festivals and picked up gig work promoting new foods such as Yerba Mate. He went through a succession of girlfriends, including a face model cum ballerina cum equestrian whose wealthy parents begged him to take her back when he dumped her for getting into a fight with his best friend's wife, even offering to pay the rent. Peg and Helen detested all of them, and especially this chain-pot-smoker ballerina who was constantly necking with Justin at the dining-room table.

The writing was now clearly on the wall that I should lay down my pen and find some other life purpose. The publishing industry in general was in free-fall with bookstores in malls and cafes vanishing as Amazon became the world's bookstore. Back when we lived in SoCal I made a habit of buying The Sunday Los Angeles Times and would lug this enormous tome into the living room and separate out its various sections, giving Justin the cartoons, Kate the travel and leisure, and then delving into the entertainment section myself, called Calendar. Being LA , emphasis was on what was happening in Hollywood, but it reviewed live theatre and books too. One Sunday I read an interview with Michael Crichton that resonated with me. He remarked that his novels were not good enough to be considered literary and were too offbeat to be bestselling commercial fiction. But then again, he had written Jurassic Park. Similarly, Peter Benchley would speak at writer's conventions about how awful his writing was. But he had written Jaws.

I submitted a couple more manuscripts but had no luck, so I went back into high-tech. First, I worked for a start-up that had come up with a way to remotely manage Linux and Unix data centres. That lasted four months, but was clearly what is known as a brain dump, and I sued them successfully to double what they had already paid me. Then I joined a start-up in San Francisco called Industrial Origami who had the rights to a patented way of bending up metal shapes, wrote them a forty-page marketing plan which terrified the CEO, who fired me. They never went anywhere. By this time Peg and I had moved to a new home in the oldest part of Morgan Hill, on the slopes of El Toro mountain with spectacular views from the backyard. Justin was just back from Malaysia where Peg had found him an internship at her company's Penang facility. I had warned him that every girl he met would want to have his baby and Kate had stocked him up with condoms and antibiotics, but even still he did get his girlfriend pregnant. Fortunately she was not a gold-digger and promptly had a walk-in abortion. We met her later because after Justin left she became a flight attendant with Singapore Airlines and got onto the San Francisco route to keep seeing him. They had bought a scooter and a surfboard and toured the whole of Bali together but the trans-Pacific relationship became too much and they both moved on.

Justin and I began working on the new house, starting with the back yard. Housing values were soaring and people were using the equity in their homes as ATM machines to finance kitchen remodels, bathroom remodels and a new trend, outdoor living rooms. Stainless steel built-in grills with a whole range of drawers and cabinets became the centre-pieces of outdoor kitchens, even outdoor living rooms with weatherproof upholstery. We set to work to demolish an old rotten gazebo and I designed an outdoor bar and countertops that could seat ten and ran natural gas, power and running water to it. For at least six months of the year we could cook and eat and drink wine here, under a huge trellis, with lights and loudspeakers, next to the pool, with a view clear across Coyote Valley and all of Morgan Hill to Lake Anderson and Finlay Ridge. The alpenglows were spectacular as the sun set and the moonrises were magical.

To build this structure we used metal studs and sills, then skinned it with backer-board. I tiled the top of it and we began to eat outdoors every day: grilled chicken, grilled salmon, grilled swordfish, tri-tips, skewered shrimp, pork loins, beer can chickens, even pineapple can game hens, with every kind of salad we could imagine. A business idea began to take shape and I made some three-dimensional models of a range of basic shapes. I took it to a designer and explained what I wanted. We needed pre-punched studs of various lengths with a universal corner joint that could be assembled using a twenty dollar pop rivet gun. I found a sheet metal company nearby whose owner wanted in on this. We made three prototypes - a module with a bartop, one without a bartop, and one that was made to support a drop-in grill.

That year the annual trade show of the Hearth, Patio and Barbecue Association was being held in Salt Lake City. I booked a small booth, lashed the modules to our little trailer, hitched it to my Mercedes SUV and drove for two days across the freezing Sierras and on east across the Nevada badlands and the Utah salt flats and dragged my three babies into position. As with all of these trade shows there were committees who walked about and nominated new products for awards. We won best new outdoor product and then Best In Show. It was a clean sweep and I was on TV next day, returning to a heroes welcome and friends keen to invest. Fresco Frames was born.

We sold the frames as Ikea type flat-packs on line, and advertised to local landscape contractors many of whom saw this as a new way of building kitchen islands and wanted our help to construct them. We became licensed contractors and hired our own crew, our little business chugged along, and we even became dealers for a range of grills and stainless steel cabinets ourselves and pitched full turnkey solutions at local street fairs. We were featured on three backyard makeover reality TV shows. The first two were for the show Yard Crashers which was produced nearby, where the host accosted people in the parking lot of Home Depot and offered to redo their yard for free in just two days.

The third was for the show Indoors Out. This was produced out of Boston, hosted by two local stone masons, but they wanted to do a celebrity special at the ranch of country singer Trace Adkins just outside Nashville, Tennessee. At first I thought that would be impractical as these shows paid nothing, just the publicity. Trace had famously been shot through the heart by his second wife but survived. He was now on his third wife, Rhonda, and she contacted me to say she would pay for a second food preparation island because one of her kids had special diet needs. Added to that I had a friend in Nashville, another musician, who offered to help me build this, so I would just need to fly out myself and ship the parts.

This was a big project so we were being given a whole three days. The ranch turned out to be Trace's personal hideout and this outdoor room was being added because Rhonda was having nothing to do with his filthy barn of a man-cave. He was six foot ten, which made the rest of us feel like hobbits when we walked past his workbenches, which he had built himself. Nashville was great and we toured around including the bar where Trace had been discovered and signed to his first recording contract. But dark clouds were once again forming and in two-thousand eight the housing bubble burst which ushered in a recession. The luxury of an outdoor room faded from most people's minds as they lost their jobs and then their homes. We needed to adapt, and quickly.

I sold Fresco Frames for pennies on the dollar to an Australian company, and we became Fresco Solar. Green living had replaced outdoor living. There were federal tax credits, utility rebates, and in San Francisco yet another subsidy, to install photovoltaic, solar thermal, and even wind on your home. I passed the electrical and solar contractor exams, and we booked home shows and street fairs to tout our renewable energy capabilities. I attended various training classes and we forged relationships with the dominant distributors. Our order book filled up with solar projects.

Helen had returned to Santa Cruz where she found work at the local print shop and soon learned to operate the Heidelberg SpeedMaster offset printer, which could spit out just about anything. She became an expert on card stock and could counterfeit any concert ticket which was a lucrative sideline for her until The Catalyst and other venues wised up and began installing scanners. She decided to move to Ireland for a while and Kate bought her a ticket to go stay with her own mother. This didn't last very long as grandma Flynn just spent all day in bed watching TV and drinking vodka, then walked downtown to eat at Lawlor's Hotel, having vowed never to cook in her own kitchen again after grandad Flynn died. Helen moved in with Dad and Finbarr.

Dad fawned over Helen who he clearly saw as the reincarnation of Mom. He drove her everywhere, dropped her off at Dublin airport to go to Paris couch-surfing, and waited up for her to get home after her waitress shifts at the K Club, a bottle of white wine ready for her on the mantelpiece. She made friends with the other staff, not the Irish who all married and settled, but the Polish girls and the French chefs, who all agreed that the worst of the worst of customers were the the English who were loud, rude, and entitled.

She moved in with the pastry chef from Bordeaux and bounced around Europe with him. He wanted to marry her, but that was not to be, and she eventually dumped him and came home.

Helen pleaded with me to try harder with my father and warned me I would regret it if I did not make amends with him. I vacillated as I did not want to ruin what was obviously a great relationship between the two of them, and who was I to say that even though he had been an awful father he was not a great grandfather. Helen had as sunny a disposition as Mom, lit up the room, had an easy laugh, and was perpetually in good humour, though there wasn't the same naïveté about her, she just liked to be on good terms with us all. Finbarr was now pushing fifty, still single, with no kids, and he too doted on Helen.

Finbarr was an extremely likable, gentle, kind, handsome, athletic person. He hiked and surfed and sailed and he was as I have said by far the most erudite of us. He was always reading and was drawn to authors such as Umberto Eco and Günter Grass. He would go into Dublin to listen to jazz or ethnic music or to see the latest indecipherable art film. He was truly an intellectual with an endless curiosity for fringe culture. He was generous and he liked women. He had been unlucky in love several times but that was about to change. He began going out with Jennifer Molloy, a gorgeous redhead from Malahide.

Then Finbarr landed a job building a motorway around Doha, capital of Qatar. The Irish economy was still in tatters and construction particularly so. The Celtic Tiger had long since thrown himself off the Cliffs of Moher never to be seen again so it would have been foolhardy not to take this offer. The lovers were undeterred by the distance. They met in Prague, in Budapest, in Belgrade. They went scuba-diving in the Canary Islands. And then they got engaged and announced a wedding the Sunday after Easter, twenty-thirteen, which would be the first time the family would all be together since the funeral eleven years earlier.

It had taken a full ten of those eleven years to finally reach agreement with the rest of the family on purchasing the headstone for Mom's grave. Dad had persisted with the notion that she would not have cared, one more last act of sadistic control or perhaps some narcissistic revenge for the fact that she had died at all and left him alone to fend for himself. But the wedding went off smoothly, with Michael as best man. Peg, ever the better judge of character than me, after this second meeting with Janet said that she was a very likable person. Jennifer's Dad gave a glowing toast to his daughter praising all of her endeavours and especially her work with Romanian orphans. Our Dad never said a word.

Michael and Janet left the next day, as did Peg, but the rest of us stayed on to discuss what would happen next. Dad no longer drove so leaving him in that house seemed like a cruel end even for him. Finbarr was in Qatar indefinitely, and neither Johannesburg nor California were practical options. That just left Connecticut. I talked to Mary and Anne about it and at first they were wary and I wondered if this was very unfair to ask of them. But when I explained to them that the mortgage balance after fourteen years of payments could not be all that big and had only originally been for half the value of the house anyway such that even after paying Michael back his long-standing stake there would be a substantial sum left and that they could use that to pay themselves back for whatever they did they soon came around.

We met with Dermot Fullam, who informed me that any woman I had ever co-habited with could pursue me for their share and then we met with John O'Reilly and had him come up with a price and put it on the market. It sold quickly and my sisters made good on relocating him with all his worldly goods to New London where they installed him in a rented house with Layla and her four kids, two each from two absent fathers. The rent, of course, was paid from Dad's money, but perhaps this was some atonement for the past. In any event I was hugely grateful for this outcome which effectively relieved me of any further responsibility for the care of my elderly father who, no matter what my feelings were, or what he had or had not done, I could never in good conscience just abandon. He was a doddering old man of eighty-four years and his daughters were making their mother proud now by ensuring he would live out his waning years in comfort surrounded by his family.

Chapter Twenty-Four. 2012 - 2022.

◇ Whack for the hurra dance your partner

round the floor ye trotters shake
isn't it the truth I tell you

lots of fun at Finnegan's wake ◇

The year before we moved Dad to Connecticut, unaware that this was imminent, we brought him over for Christmas. I was dreading it but it went smoothly enough. One of our holiday staples was taco bar, where we made seasoned beef and chicken, and laid out soft and crispy tacos, shredded cheese, tomatoes, lettuce, sour cream, taco sauce and everyone filed along loading their plate to their liking. Peg's kids were there. Kelly, now twenty-one, was home from Cal Poly where she was a biology major. Dad pulled his usual stunt of pretending to be helpless and Kelly kindly helped him through the process of assembling his Mexican meal.

Helen bounded in the door as we were about to eat and it was as though someone had sprinkled pixie dust in the air. Dad's gait lengthened and his back straightened and he couldn't wait to sit next to her and answer all her questions. Next day Helen and I took him to Satori, one of our favourite local wineries, where he bantered ceaselessly, endlessly repeating that if they had anything like this in Ireland no-one would ever do a day's work, but all in all it was a tolerable visit and when we packed him off back east I felt every bit the good son.

A couple of years later, making good on my promise to morally support my sisters, I found that they had installed him in a very cosy and obviously expensive independent living facility. The small towns of East Lyme and New London, where they all lived, lie very close to the seaside town of Niantic, and we organized a beach barbecue for everyone that summer, pulling Dad across the beach in a wheelchair with enormous wheels like a moon buggy. I suspected it would be the last such outing of his life.

Mary explained that she had moved all of his money into a bank account in her name and because of this the state was obligated to pay for everything. She knew how to work the system, and she had likewise filled out all the paperwork to obtain permanent disability for Rex, because of his head injury all those years ago. She explained that because Rex was so intelligent people did not notice how he struggled with organizing simple tasks, couldn't multi-task at all, and missed social cues. And she had done all of this with no help whatsoever from her long estranged ex-husband.

The following year Helen and I flew over for Easter, to find they had already moved him into an assisted living facility. We took him out to a fancy seafood restaurant in Mystic. He had a lot of trouble getting in and out of the car, but he noticed the big coffee table book I was carrying and asked about it as we waited for our table. Long, long ago, when he and Ena were at the zenith of their business success, he took on a consulting assignment that caused him to have to commute to the tiny hamlet of Clara in county Offaly, just west of the county seat, Tullamore, itself a town known only to the outside world for its eponymous whiskey. Somewhere, on one of the paved-over goat trails that traverse this long forsaken corner of the vast bog that is politely referred to as the Irish midlands, Dad stopped at a petrol station and noticed a four-bladed wooden airplane propellor hanging on the wall inside the derelict repair shop. He enquired about it but its provenance was lost in the mists of time, so he bought it and set it up in our hallway like some strange lopsided crucifix, or Katanga cross.

His brother, Uncle Michael, who fancied himself as an aviation expert, did some research and discovered that, four-bladed wooden propellors being something of an oddity, it was almost certainly from a World War One RE8 biplane. He made a note of the serial number and wrote to the Imperial War Museum, who replied that it was more likely from a twin-engined Vickers Vimy, the world's first long range bomber that had come into service just as the war ended. This captured the imagination of the whole family, for we all knew that the very first trans-Atlantic flight in nineteen-nineteen, by Alcock and Brown, in a Vickers Vimy, had crash-landed in a bog in Galway and what were the odds that this was not one of the propellors of that very plane that Dad had discovered only a stone's throw away?

Whether or not any of this was true this particular propellor had now crossed the Atlantic at least three times and was now stored in Mary's garage. The book I had with me that night was a compendium of famous flights that I had found in the book store of a local air museum, and the cover image was a painting that depicted Brown climbing out on the wing of the famous plane to de-ice one of the engines and there was that same four-bladed propellor. The point of this exercise was to let themall know that although I seldom saw them they were ever-present in my thoughts but to what extent I succeeded I will never know.

Peg exhorted me to bring Dad over for one last Christmas, which we did in twenty-sixteen. This was a disaster and it was entirely my fault. I picked him up at San Francisco airport where they had lost his luggage, so he was already in full victim mode. It infuriated me and all my rage that he had lived on for so long after being so instrumental as I still saw it in Mom's untimely death came rushing back. He had not one iota of remorse, not just for that but for me, for Ena, for Mary, nothing. And he had suffered zero consequence for any of it and just lived on and on and on, taken care of one way or another by all of us.

I remembered the Christmas when I was eight and Santa brought me and Michael the Scalextric set. We were two deliriously excited little boys chomping at the bit to race the slot cars around the track, but the set came with a transformer that had no plug, just bare wires, and only Dad knew how to attach the plug and he was still in bed. He finally came downstairs and wired up the transformer and plugged it in. I immediately squeezed the thumb grip on the throttle and my little race car shot forward, came to the first curved track and took off into the air hitting Dad in the face. He roared at me, purple faced, and I dashed out of the room and up the stairs in terror.

The next three days at our lovely home in Morgan Hill were hell, not just for me, but because of me for everyone. I stayed in bed for as long as I could, then got up and drank wine until I passed out again in a new stupor, then repeated this until he finally left. I might have been unfaithful to my wife but he was a self-confessed bigamist. And I was not screwing my wife one minute and her sister the next. I knew that what I had done was wrong and when the opportunity presented itself years later on a river excursion into the Malaysian rain forest, I resisted the temptation to have sex with a very willing and very beautiful fellow Apple employee. I had experienced remorse and stupidly believed this was a universal human emotion. The very notion of atonement was anathema to my father. He had duped my mother into taking him back after she had finally worked up the courage to leave him, and now she was long dead while he was apparently immortal, impervious to guilt and shame and whatever health issues the stress of such negative feelings might bring on the rest of us.

Finbarr and Jennifer now had two small boys, Phillip and Lawrence, and announced plans to visit Connecticut the following summer. Helen booked us an AirBnB on the beach in Niantic and I flew her, Justin, and his pregnant girlfriend, Sage, over to spend a few days with all of them. Mary and Anne still had their sailboat moored at a dock outside the ramshackle house where Kevin still lived after they split up and we sailed it down the river, underneath the Amtrak bascule bridge and across the bay to beach it at our house. Dad was now wheelchair bound and incapable of leaving the nursing home but the weather was good enough that we could wheel him around the grounds. Hilary's kids came over from Long Island on the ferry and we had such a wild beach-barbecue party, drinking all of the homeowner's booze, that Helen was permanently barred from AirBnB and we forfeited our deposit.

On January twenty-ninth, twenty-eighteen my grandson, Kian Reef Kenny, was born, and a few weeks later we received word that Dad was failing fast. We all gathered at Mary's rambling colonial era home in East Lyme with its huge fireplace that even had a nook in the chimney that had been used as part of the underground railroad to hide runaway slaves. And then we stood around his bedside for that final vigil. Social workers asked if we would like a pastor present to pray with us, and we assured them that we were all born again atheists with no interest in any such succour. He lay there motionless until at some unknown moment he ceased to breathe, his heart stopped beating, and he just expired.

I felt nothing. I wanted to hate him but what was there left to hate? In fact, I hated myself for not having the slightest glimmer of filial love left in my heart. But this was the truth. This man, who had inflicted so much pain on those around him, had felt none himself. It was impossible to feel sorry for him. He had waltzed through life deaf to all criticism, heedless of the suffering of others, and immune to all illness. It was impossible to view his passing as any kind of loss, for myself, for the rest of my family, or his family, or the whole of mankind. To be sure it closed yet another chapter in my life but a far brighter one had just begun. I was now a grandfather myself.

Peg and I were in a bad place that summer. Though I had long since paid off all of our investors, with enough left over to treat myself to a Porsche, I had taken on some projects that I should have foreseen would be trouble. I had taken out what are called zombie loans, short term cash infusions that gobbled up the margins on our projects. It took a toll, but in the end we decided we could weather it. To turn the page we went up to San Francisco to see Hamilton and I have never seen a more ravishing Peg in an evening dress and heels, bare arms sculpted from her kickboxing workouts, and then we drove on to Bodega Bay, went kayaking, hiked along the cliffs, ate oysters and bought an oil painting. We stayed in a cabin on the water and dined in the little town's best restaurant, ordering the sole, but laughing that it was almost certainly tilapia.

And then disaster struck. Peg was diagnosed with stage four lung cancer. I had never known anyone to survive this and all of us struggled with the possibility of her oncoming death. I did not know how to be around her as I watched her hair fall out in clumps when she showered. But the chemotherapy worked, the one tiny metastasis on her brain was caught in time, and with the tumour reduced in size she underwent surgery that took hours longer than planned but was successful. I drove her back and forth to immunotherapy for the next couple of years and she made a full recovery.

After Dad's death I had a strange epiphany. My animosity toward Michael just evaporated. Going back to my teenage years I had bought into Ena's belief that Michael and Mary were the bane of my parents' existence. Even though I should have seen later that this was rich coming from the arch-home wrecker herself I never shook it off. I eventually relented where Mary was concerned but Michael had no excuse. But now, wherever such sibling rivalries spring from, this psychological construct, this emotional baggage, was lifted. Maybe it was tied to some spark of hope in me that went out with my father's ending.

I resolved to travel to South Africa and mend my fences with Michael. And then as I was researching this trip Covid hit. We were now all on lockdown and the pandemic would linger in Africa long after we all started to be vaccinated here. I used the ensuing economic meltdown as a smoke-screen to finally pull the plug on my business and went to work as a project manager for a much larger solar company, steering a slate of projects all the way from handoff to completion. This was an easy remote job and so in August of twenty twenty-one I was able to fly over to Connecticut to stay with Anne and see everyone. Broadway was just coming back and we went to see a play about an epidemic of blindness which you sat through in the dark wearing headphones. I met Anne's new boyfriend, Billy, and we took Layla's two younger girls kayaking around the wetlands, watching the ospreys feeding their young on the pole-top nests that had been erected everywhere for them. On the weekdays I worked West Coast hours, from about ten to seven. They might have a paltry choice of wines in Connecticut, and both of my sisters had long since become teetotallers so it didn't bother them, but they have far better seafood than we had, and I devoured the fried clams and lobster rolls and crab cakes and clam chowder. It was a great visit and long overdue.

The following year I finalized my South Africa trip. I read a five-hundred page history of the country, a biography of Nelson Mandela, Nadine Gordimer's Burger's Daughter about apartheid, and guides to San Bushman rock art and South African wines. I studied an enormous map and began to put together an itinerary. I consulted Michael about when was the best time to go and he suggested October, both because this was their spring when the foliage is just coming back so it is easier to see the animals and because we could make use of their time share at a game reserve then. I booked my plane ticket which was surprisingly cheap because tourism had not yet rebounded from the pandemic.

Finbarr and Jennifer had moved back to Ireland, bought a house and were both working. They too were anxious to do some post-Covid travel and announced they were going to Connecticut that summer. Even though I had just been over the prior year the chance to see them all was too much to resist so I set out to repeat what I had done again. I took a red-eye that dropped me into Minneapolis in the small hours and then on to Hartford to arrive about noon. There was a text from Mary to tell me Rex was going to pick me up, a last-minute change that I thought nothing of at the time.

Sure enough Rex rolled up to the terminal in his old black convertible with the top down. There was a young girl in the car with him, Tanya, who I would have put at about thirteen, whose presence he didn't explain. My initial thought was that he was babysitting her. She slept in the back seat all the way to Anne's house. They dropped me off and left and I went upstairs to take a nap having had no sleep on the flight over. I came back down later to find everyone pottering around. It had been five years since I had seen Phillip and Laurence, other than on WhatsApp and Zoom, and the toddlers I remembered were now polite ten and eight year olds respectively. Jennifer coaxed them to eat their dinners and I started an episode of *Star Wars - Strange New Worlds* on my laptop for them, then paused it until they finished.

The visit followed much the same pattern as the previous year but I did take one day off to go into New York City where we took the boys to the American Museum of Natural History, which is all about the dinosaurs. Later, Mary, Anne, my grandniece, Cura and I went to see *Book of Mormon* on Broadway. Anne's house was crowded with all of us the first week, but Finbarr and family moved to the old timeshare that we had inherited from Mom and Dad for the second week and we mostly socialized there at the beach or in the pool. We visited Mystic Aquarium one day, which I was able to finesse without taking off work and I introduced the boys to Dippin' Dots and paid for bait so they could feed the cow-nose rays.

However, there was one glaring difference this time. Tanya, it turned out, was eighteen years old, and Rex, now forty-one years old, was her boyfriend. I asked Mary about this and she told me that Tanya had been staying in John Harney's basement on Long Island and that she had come onto Rex while he was there doing some house painting. She came from a really abusive background and that was what girls like that did. It was a real problem because Rex was not allowed to have visitors at his subsidized apartment and ran the risk of being evicted. She also produced an email from a therapist saying that it was possible that Rex had arrested emotional development going back to the night of the accident and that was why he was attracted to her.

This all struck me as very strange. I had brought over a couple of new board games and one night we set up *Ticket To Ride* on Anne's dining room table. Rex, Layla's two younger girls, Finbarr and myself played. This is a strategy game where you try to build out the longest railroad. It is easy to learn and play and in fact one of the younger girls won her very first time. Rex tried to explain to Tanya what was going on but she obviously did not understand. Instead she uncoiled his man-bun and re-braided it. At Water's Edge someone took a photo of the two of them together in the hot tub and Rex posted it on Facebook. On WhatsApp Rex posted that they were staying in a motel in Groton and going bowling and wanted to know if any of us wanted to join them.

Another night Anne and I were hanging out in her kitchen around ten in the evening, so I called Peg for a chat to find that Helen was with her and they were about to Doordash themselves a meal. I gave them a rundown on the Rex and Tanya affair and both of them were horrified. Anne chimed in that it was really John Harney's fault for allowing Tanya to be there in the first place. Helen took her at her word and proceeded to lambast John on LinkedIn the next day for grooming this girl for his son. And that, by the time I got home, had produced an avalanche of back and forth emails that revealed an entirely different story, going back all the way to that bitter parting on Saba two decades and counting earlier.

Chapter Twenty-Five. 2022 - Present Day.

'Twill out, 'twill out. I peace?
No, I will speak as liberal as the north.
Let heaven and men and devils, let 'em all,
All, all cry shame against me, yet I'll speak.

Emilia
Othello Act V, Scene 2, lines 226-228

Tanya lived on the same street as John and his wife Janet in the town of Kings Park on Long Island. She and her older brother were two Russian orphans who had been adopted by an abusive couple as infants and been raised by two severe hoarders, a stepfather who masturbated in front of them and was violent and a stepmother who had drunk herself to death. They were routinely in and out of shelters or holed up in the trailer in the driveway. Someone had tried to rape Tanya when her vagina was still so small he couldn't fit. She had to wear diapers at night because she constantly wet the bed. Janet, together with several other mothers on the street, did whatever they could to help. This included inviting these two children to family gatherings over the years from the time they were young children such that they became friendly with John's close-in-age grandchildren Trott and Cura. Helen apologized profusely to John and Janet as she read their long and highly detailed descriptions of what had really occurred. I was reading them too, my first communication with Janet ever and with John since our altercation after the millennium dive over two decades earlier.

John even produced a photo taken one Christmas of seven year old Tanya sitting on a couch in his home with Rex standing behind her, leering at the camera. As soon as she turned eighteen and could flee her stepfather they allowed her to move into their basement while they helped her to acquire her citizenship papers, long since lost in the severe hoarding house, from when she was adopted from Russia, get her adult ed driving lessons, acquire a car, a couple of part-time jobs ,and secure a New York State paid-for dog-grooming course two nights a week which lasted over seven months and provided a State Certification. And this was where Rex found her, and Rex, who had known Tanya since childhood, knew all about her background. He swore to

186

John and Janet that he would stay away from her because she would indeed throw herself at him if he sent the wrong signal. And for the next few months all seemed well.

Then one day one of the other mothers who cared for Tanya saw Rex's black convertible parked outside the local no-tell motel Tanya and surreptitiously took some photos. Tanya then confided to one of the women who was in the car pool that drove Tanya to dog grooming school thirty minutes from Kings Park that she had been involved in a sexual relationship with Rex and that he drove to John's home to pick her up in the middle of the night to go to said local dive motel. Then the mothers confiscated Tanya's phone and discovered hundreds of photos and videos of Rex and Tanya sexting back and forth dating back to his visit just after she turned eighteen as well as naked photos from their meet-ups in hotels on Long Island. It was now the spring of twenty twenty-two and an apparently contrite Tanya at first agreed to stop all this, even calling Rex a pedophile herself, but a few weeks later ran off with Rex.

John alerted Mary and Anne to all of this and they apparently agreed that this was wrong and Anne sent an email saying unambiguously that she did not condone it and that they would not be welcome together in her home. This was where I came in and I am quite certain that my sisters made that last minute switch in who was picking me up at the airport to somehow normalize all of this, to pull me in from the outset. If I had known then what I know now I probably would not have made the trip. I even tried to reason with Rex after I came home. I sent him a copy of *The Deepest Well*, the book by California Surgeon General Nadine Harris about treating the long-term effects of childhood abuse. He read it and answered my questions but it had no effect.

Mary, a licensed therapist employed by the child services department of the state of Connecticut, displayed zero empathy for Tanya. In the two weeks I was there she never once uttered her name and when the subject did come up she fretted that if the girl did leave Rex he might have a breakdown or even a seizure. To her, Rex was a completely blameless victim, incapable because of his traumatic brain injury of understanding the harm in any of this and therefore by her convoluted logic was not doing anything wrong. Anne, as was typical for her, waded into the matter and made light of the risk factors in Doctor Nadine's book. Never mind that this is established science and that you can now find the ten question ACE (adverse childhood experience) quiz all over the internet including on the CDC website. Tanya experienced eight or nine of these which unquestioningly means she lives with a level of toxic stress that will greatly shorten her life expectancy unless she receives major and ongoing treatment.

Tanya is physically, mentally and emotionally underdeveloped. I have only to compare her behaviour at age eighteen with that of my own daughter, my stepdaughter, and their peers to see how utterly lost she is. I am ashamed of the very small part I played in socializing with the pair of them although I have subsequently left Rex in no doubt as to my total disapproval as have his father and stepmother. But it is pointless as long as his mother and aunt have his back and enable their relationship as they have done for the past two years. It is like the old child-rearing conundrum: if one parent tells you that you cannot have ice-cream unless you eat your vegetables and the other gives you the ice-cream anyway what do you grow up to be?

The argument that Rex cannot be held accountable because of his brain injury and his resulting executive brain function defectiveness holds no water with me. First of all, as I have recounted, Rex displayed sociopathic tendencies long before this injury - Yosemite, Hootie and The Blowfish, disregard for his dying grandmother - and it can easily be argued that riding a lawnmower down a hill at high speed into a wall was not the cause of his problems but just a predictable result of the fact that he was already a rampant drug-addled narcissist. And subsequent to this blow to his head he earned a four- year college degree, held down numerous jobs, including as a technician installing climate controls in hotels in Florida and Hawaii, and has had plenty of girlfriends his own age.

Tanya lived a two-and-a-half-hour drive from him and Rex routinely made the journey including booking the hotel and spiriting her away in the dark and successfully concealed this from everyone for nine months. That seems to me to display a very high level of executive brain function. But Rex, being a sociopath, with the help of his enabling therapist mother, has fooled the system and now he never has to work a day in his life again because our taxes pay what he arrogantly refers to as his "state wages". To round this out, Mary has now persuaded the powers that be that Tanya is autistic so that she too is on permanent disability. Not only are they now slowly killing this girl by ignoring her psychological needs, subjugating her to the sexual desires of a narcissistic monster, but they have removed any possibility of her ever leading a purpose-driven life.

Going back to that night in The Merriman Hotel in Kinvara when we were all just about to learn of Rex's accident and Mary flared up and stormed off at my assertion that living in a cabin the woods in the middle of nowhere was a derelict path for an educated woman, she had done it again. She bought a six hundred square foot fixer upper on the Vermont-Canada border an hour and a half from the nearest Home Depot. And now she has moved Rex and Tanya in next door, a forty-two year old man and his twenty year old concubine. She has had them working on renovating her home, which she and her boyfriend Dan pay them for. What possible good outcome is there here even if the weather doesn't do them all in?

Anne, in one of her many unhinged theories, blames John for Rex's accident. He should not have left his eighteen-year-old son alone in America with all the car keys while he went off to celebrate his fortieth birthday in Ireland. So far as I know most lawnmowers do not have ignition keys, and would the result not have been the very same if Mary had just taken John down to the city for the weekend for dinner and a show? And does this mean that Mom and Dad are responsible for Michael's car crash all those years ago? And so on. Rex is responsible for his actions and no one else.

Mary and Anne had for years led me to believe that John had no contact of any kind with his children or grandchildren and did nothing for them. They knew that I had zero contact with John and for that matter no motivation to question what they were saying. But now the Berlin Wall had come tumbling down. At first this led to an email exchange about how much or how little they had told me but this soon descended into a debate about whether I just did not remember what they had told me because they had told me late at night after I had been drinking. That now escalated into the assertion that I had started drinking at lunchtime every day and was an alcoholic like my Aunt Hilary, who had drowned in her swimming pool in The Hamptons from complications due to alcoholism.

I was flummoxed by all of this and even sat down to review the entire two weeks in Niantic. The first day I had simply slept all day. On eight of the other week days I had worked until seven in the evening when a few times I did borrow a car and dash to the liquor store before it closed by law at eight. On the day in New York they well knew I had my first glass of wine while buying them dinner. On one weekend we played with the boys in the pool until it closed at sunset and on the other I kayaked with Anne one day and then had an afternoon massage with Mary the next. Yes, I drink a lot of red wine, it's one of the perks of where we live, but, unlike Hilary, no doctor has ever told me to stop. So why was Mary making this up? And even more bizarre, why was Anne buying into it when she knew, because I stayed at her house, that this lunchtime drinking was a fantasy? This was the first time in my life that my sisters had methodically turned against me. I had always supported them and enjoyed the times we spent together. Clearly there was an undercurrent of resentment all along that had now bubbled to the surface. And then finally I understood. This was the first time I had ever challenged their highly self-righteous view of the world and, since they did not drink, alcohol was my Achilles Heel.

I now learned that an exchange with Anne was like throwing a lighted match into a box of fireworks. She would explode into a cacophony of gibberish. But at least she spoke or wrote her pretzel thoughts, unlike her older sister, who would embark on character assassination by a thousand cuts, with much of the stabbing done by her surrogates, her useful idiots, in Vladimir Lenin's parlance, narcissistic Rex, clueless Layla and self-appointed moral arbiter Anne. Mary and Anne behaved like a pair of all-knowing goddesses on Mount Olympus. Like Athene or Hera they flew down to meddle in the lives of the lesser mortals, to pay the deposit on yet another apartment for Layla and the two girls, to take Cura to the Smithsonian in pursuit of her goal of becoming an astronaut, or to take the two younger girls to some theme park to take their minds off the ever-present fear of once again becoming homeless.

Anne moved in with Billy to leave her twenty-two year old daughter, twenty-year old son and eighteen year old grand-nephew to live in the house she had bought a few years earlier, with its stairs with no handrail and its duct-taped faucets in the downstairs shower. Uncle Tony had once remarked that Dad never asked a question to which he did not already know the answer and at the time its significance escaped me. Here was the same thing in my sisters - unless the thought sprang whole from within their own heads it could not be imparted to them. The dry drunks knew more than anyone else. To them we were now all just vexations to their oh-so-temperate spirits. Hubble, bubble, toil and trouble, as they brewed and then distilled and then served up their own reality. As Dad was wont to say: my mind is made up so don't confuse me with the facts.

What they had created was a crazy web of codependent relationships for which the better analogy would be found in Alice In Wonderland. Anne was like The Queen of Hearts. Kevin, her ex-husband was to blame. Off with his head. John was to blame for Rex. Off with his head. Nic, father of Trott and Cura, was to blame for the fact that they refused to have any contact with their mother. Off with his head. And now I had dared to question the morality of Rex and Tanya. Off with my head. And Mary was The Red Queen herself, forever running around but getting nowhere. Her trip around the world with her stint in a Buddhist monastery, her odyssey around the country in her boyfriend's converted bus that ran on biodiesel and solar, and her drive through Boston that she had described to Peg as if it were the zombie apocalypse when she was picking up some furniture for her cabin in the woods.

They had pulled their whole families swirling down the rabbit hole with them leaving none of them independent and whole. And for a long time they had fooled me too. As I thought back on the many times they had told me that John had bolted to take up with his new American wife, who his own family hated, and never be seen or heard from again, I realized that it was always one on one, with none of their kids listening, usually driving around, because they knew full well that out of the mouths of one of those babes might come the truth. I confronted John and Janet with what I had been told and a torrent of photos and dates of holiday gatherings and summer pool parties came back to me in email after email going back to when John had bought Layla her first car.

They had a perfectly normal relationship with Rex and Layla and the four grandchildren. I go for months at a time without seeing my adult children, becoming closer in times of crisis, being pro-active about visiting my grandson, and always planning some holiday get-together. They are independent adults with their own lives and jobs and relationships. We don't go about our lives like some endless Mad Hatter's tea party. The lopsided story that had lasted for over two decades was now suddenly set straight and John, Janet, Peg and I maintained a regular exchange of news and views about our families from then on. John freely admitted he had been a dick back on Saba and we all readily shrugged it off as water under the bridge or over the dam, or whatever, but an incident long since superseded by our rich and busy exploits ever since. With growing confidence that this was a healthy, honest relationship with John and Jan I began to wonder what else was not what I had always thought it was.

I asked John about the night Mary threw herself in the canal but he told me he had not been there. However, he found the mobile phone number of Eddie Mullen, the person who had rescued Mary that night long ago from the canal and exchanged a couple of texts with him. I did not know Eddie, but I knew his sister Mary very well, because she was the same Mary Mullen that had worked for us all those years ago. This was a reliable witness. Eddie was adamant that Mary had fallen in high as a kite on who knows what drugs, maybe trying to walk or jump to the far side and he was equally sure that if he had not fished her out she would have been, as he put it, a goner, but not because that was the outcome she sought. Eddie's description to John was that he was working on the roof of the corner house by the canal when he heard a splash that sounded like someone diving in, but then didn't hear anything else, so, he stood up and looked over and saw a person face down in the canal, not swimming. He ran over, jumped in himself, and pulled her out. John has even produced a visual diagram - see below. According to him, Mary told him as follows: "Bren and I were down smoking hash by the canal. I got really stoned and saw some ducks on the other side of the canal and was going over to them, not thinking about the fact that there was all this water in front of me. I just kept walking and ended up in the water."

That night Eddie called the home of Linda Lyons, Mary's bestie, and Linda and her brother, Jack, came and took Mary back to the Lyons residence. Linda's parents were so shocked by Mary's condition they felt they had no choice but to bring her home immediately. There was no denying Mary had almost drowned and I can only imagine Mom's consternation that some person had called the Lyonses instead of her and now the whole episode would be the talk of Naas for weeks to come. Mary knew she was in serious trouble so it was an obvious ploy to claim she was so depressed by all the problems in her own life that she had decided to end it. But what could those problems be? Mom and I had a standing joke that we were all deprived of a deprived upbringing. On the surface Mary had a great life, was a gorgeous popular blonde, able to lord it with her Dublin sophistication over the lifelong denizens of Naas as I had done a few years earlier. She had clothes, money, a circle of girlfriends. She sailed and went on foreign holidays, and she had brains to boot. What had happened to her?

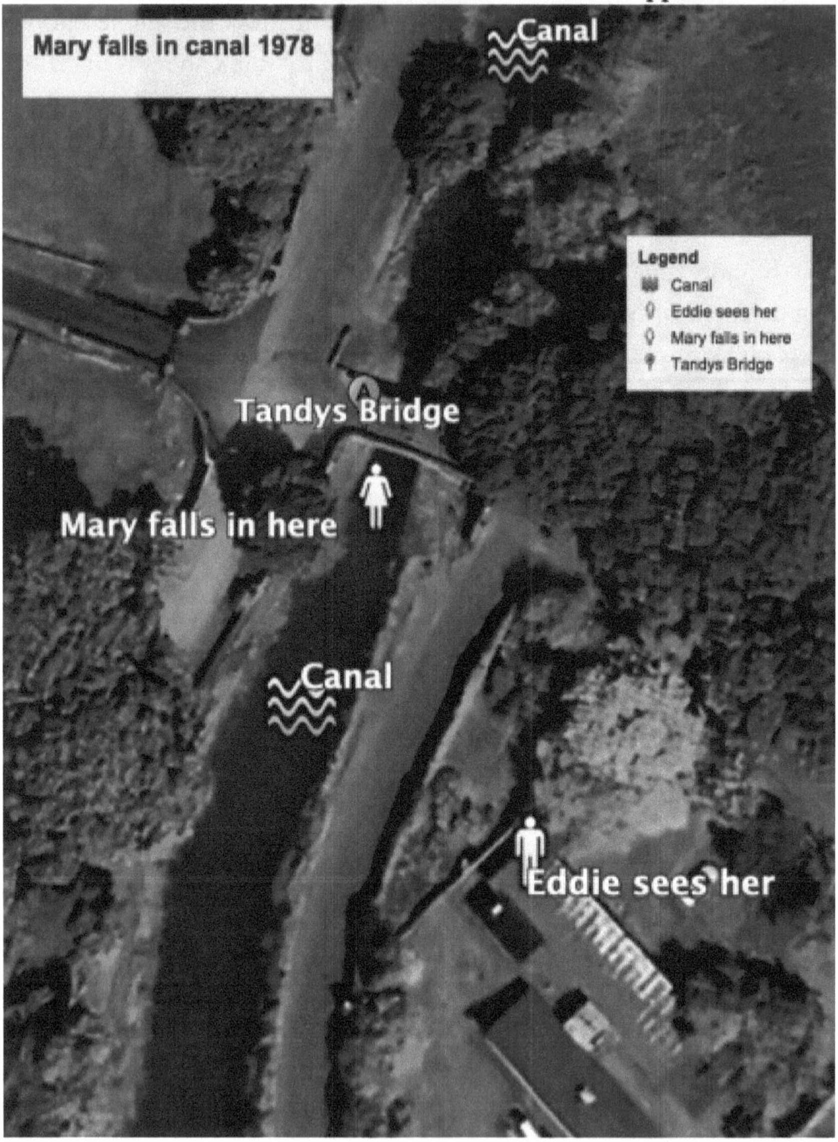

Grand Canal, Naas branch, Ireland

Chapter Twenty-Six. Present Day.

And the truth shall set you free.

Jesus of Nazareth

Mary had told Mom she had tried to kill herself, Mom had believed her, and I had believed Mom. It was a staggering act of self-serving behaviour and one that Mary never, ever recanted. Plus, this was the inciting incident that had led me to believe she had been sexually abused by Dad. Based on this whopping revelation was any of it true? Was my whole life just the butterfly effect of my narcissistic, conniving teenage sister? Mary had told Kate that she had recovered a memory of sexual abuse under hypnotherapy and Kate, a nurse who had worked extensively with sexually abused women, felt she had to give this some credence. Kate had believed Mary and I had believed Kate.

Mary went ahead with her accusatory letter to Dad. Now, at that time, there was a bestseller going around called *The Courage To Heal,* which was first published in nineteen eighty-eight. To be fair this was a breakthrough guide and finally shook off the patriarchal legacy of Freud, but to quote Wikipedia: *"the book has been criticized for being used primarily by incompetent therapists, for creating in children false memories of abuse, as well as for its authors' lack of qualifications, for creating an industry which has isolated and separated family members despite having no positive proof the abuse occurred, and for destructively replacing individual identities with that of a 'survivor'. Bass and Davis have also been criticized for leaping to unwarranted, implausible conclusions with significant consequences and for scientific errors found in the first edition that were not corrected in subsequent reprintings."*

The book had the unintended consequence of spawning an entire industry of therapists who claimed they could help you recover repressed memories. That in turn had the effect of creating a reactionary movement that soon debunked the whole idea of repressed memory syndrome and came up with the idea of false memory syndrome in defence of those wrongly accused. Was Dad wrongly accused? And if so then how do we explain the fact that Mary did indeed turn her life around after this and embark on a successful career as a therapist herself?

Judith Herman, a Harvard psychiatry professor, wrote the classic book, Father-Daughter Incest, which, on re-reading it, seems to make the likelihood of this happening in our family very low. Our mother was ever-present in our home and in our lives. There was a naïveté about her however, and when she found that Kate and I were enjoying teenage sex she almost had a nervous breakdown. She cried for days and my driving privileges were revoked. Dad and her sister got away with an affair under her nose for years but there is no comparison between sex between consenting adults and the actions of a pedophile pervert. In fact, Dad's appetite for adult sex partners of itself makes it highly unlikely that he would have had any interest in child sex. Mary was no Cinderella and Mom was no wicked stepmother.

That book was a prelude to Herman's seminal work *Trauma and Recovery,* published in nineteen ninety-two and still in print which ranges across every kind of abuse. In chapter five, devoted to child abuse, she describes in great detail the conditions under which chronic child abuse occurs and the symptoms that are exhibited by the abuse victims. None of it is consistent with the home life I recall nor the behaviour then or now of any of my siblings. Two years later Elizabeth Loftus, psychologist and memory expert, along with her partner, Katherine Ketcham, published The *Myth Of Repressed Memory* whose central theme is to lay bare the fallacy that was driving the whole industry that had preyed on my suggestible sister and by extension my father. But for me the die was cast. Child sexual abuse was a persistent plague especially in closed societies such as the clergy ridden Ireland of that time.

There are other factors in Mary's personal make-up that matter here. She invents things she knows are not true when it suits her. I did not start drinking at lunchtime in Connecticut and John did not ever abandon his kids, any more than Peg did. She routinely leaps to wrong conclusions. Peg and I were not on the outs at the end of the Saba diving trip because I did not buy her an engagement ring. More recently she concluded that I had hacked Peg's phone and set up a new WhatsApp channel to eavesdrop on her. In twenty-five years I have never so much as looked inside Peg's handbag. Mary almost bought a house with two gaping holes in the roof because she thought it was priced "below market value". She has decided, without evidence, that Tanya is autistic because it suits her purpose. Per Janet Dwyer, her unofficial stepmom Katy, who lived next door to Tanya, has two autistic sons, has known Tanya since elementary school, and has also concluded she is not autistic. None of Tanya's extensive medical file which is also in Janet's possession makes any mention of autism.

My best explanation now for Mary's amazing recovery is that she was drawn to therapy because it is the ultimate attention-seeking behaviour and that she then became a therapist herself because she saw the awesome power being one had conferred on the therapist who "recovered" her memory. Moreover, the whole psychotherapy business has almost no accountability. There is no right or wrong and no life and death responsibility, just the vague manipulation of feelings. No-one is there to oversee what happens. The clients just show up and talk for an hour, pay for the privilege of being listened to, and go away again. It is the perfect occupation for someone devoid of empathy or remorse. One of the risks of being a psychotherapist is what is known as countertransference. In other words being vigilant about not allowing the patient's pain to enter one's own world. That risk is, of course, nonexistent in someone who is oblivious to the suffering of others.

Mary, whether she knew about Ena's perfidy as she was dying of cancer or not, and I doubt that she did, felt no compulsion to comfort either Ena or her mother, let alone her father whose world was also in free-fall. And two decades later she had no hesitation about depositing her brain-damaged son and uncontrollable and possibly bipolar daughter on her dying mother's doorstep while she took a trip around the world on her own with her divorce payout, having taken John Harney for every legal penny. The layers of self-deception in Mary's world have left an emotional blast radius that now spans four generations. There are her parents, her own life, that of her siblings, that of her own two children, and that of her four grand-children. And now we can add Tanya to the pyre.

Iago, the villain in Shakespeare's Othello, is the best metaphor I have yet found for Mary. Both the arc of Iago in the play and Mary in real-life are a series of improvised deceptions. Iago's wife, Emilia, figures out the truth, but too late, and he kills her before she can reveal all. Modern life is more subtle, but Mary has sought to kill my character in the eyes of anyone she can influence. It galls her that Peg will not row in behind her and turn against me. Iago's victims go far beyond his hated master, Othello, and so too with Mary. She has no more remorse for all her collateral damage, her children, her grandchildren, and unlucky step-daughter/step-grand-daughter Tanya, than Iago for dead Desdemona, Emilia and Rodrigo and maimed Cassio. And that is to say nothing of the pain she inflicted on her mother, her brothers, her uncle Tony, her ex-husband and father to her two children, and for that matter the undeserved odium heaped on Dad, over and above what he deserved, perhaps driving him over some precipice that might otherwise have left room for some reconciliation, however slight.

Chapter Twenty-Seven. 2022.

Live as if you were to die tomorrow.
Learn as if you were to live forever.

Mahatma Gandhi

I did go to Africa to visit Michael in October of twenty twenty-two. It was the trip of a lifetime for me and though I planned for it as though this was surely a one-off bucket list trip, I would return in a heartbeat. The country is vast, three times the size of France or California. A generation after the end of Apartheid there are still enormous social problems and Michael and Janet, like most middle class white people, and now middle class black and brown people, live in a house with a high wall around it, topped by a ten thousand volt electric fence. I met two of Michael's three stepchildren and his grand-daughter, Erin. All were incredibly welcoming and helpful, entertaining me the day I arrived with a braai, Afrikaans for barbecue, with ostrich and spicy local sausage, making me feel all the worse for having shunned them for so long.

I took a puddle-jumper to Kruger National Park in the east, stayed in a lodge overlooking a bend in a river that was home to a bloat of hippos, hired a safari guide who found a leopard in a tree eating an impala, then some lions, and of course elephants everywhere, too many of them. I rented a car and drove myself around taking thousands of photos with my powerful new Nikon camera, both in the park and in the mountains to the west with their spectacular waterfalls and rock formations. Then I flew back all the way to Cape Town in the southwest, where the colonization had all begun as a refuelling stop for ships coming and going to India.

Cape Town is their San Francisco, a spectacular port and beach town. I walked around safely late at night, took the cable car up Table Mountain, visited Mandela's cell on Robben island and went cage diving with sharks. I Ubered to Stellenbosch, their version of Napa or Bordeaux, where they have been making wine for well over three centuries, as Michael had asserted all those years ago. And in all my time in South Africa I never had a bad glass of wine, nor paid much more than twenty dollars a bottle in restaurants. From Cape Town I flew to Durban where I did some real scuba diving on

Aliwal Shoal, surrounded by what they call raggies and we call nurse sharks. I visited Gandhi's old house, now a museum to the Apartheid struggle, the only visitor to brave the drive into the township that morning.

I drove back to Johannesburg through the Drakensberg mountains, taking two hikes with Zulu guides, one to see some San Bushman art at Shelter Pass, said to be the images that decoded the meaning of it all - a symbiotic relationship between the San people and the Eland, Africa's largest antelope, which they both hunted and worshipped - and the other just to enjoy the incredible beauty of it all, taking photos of blooming Protea, the country's national flower along the trail, and then, to my delight, spotting a herd of hundreds of Eland below us as we ascended Baboon Rock. I stayed overnight at the small art town of Clarens, where I once again found king klip fish on the menu, second only to kudu steak as my favourite meal there, though I would never pass up a plate of oysters or a bowl of peri-peri chicken livers either.

Back in Joburg Michael rented a truck and we drove two hours north to the Pilanesberg game reserve where he and Janet have long owned a time share. Janet was once bitten by a highly venomous Mozambique spitting cobra, in the villa, and anyway was dealing with a sick animal, so it was just the two of us. This park is nestled in a volcanic crater and can be criss-crossed in a day, but it surpassed Kruger in viewing opportunities, all of the big five, half a dozen kinds of antelope, great bird-life, more great braai, wine and local beer at the lodges or on the back porch.

We chatted late into the night all four days, then returned to spend the last two days with Michael's family and friends, fitting in a day trip to the township of Soweto, more populous than Joburg proper, including a tour of the Mandela home, where Winnie lived while Nelson was incarcerated for twenty-seven years. We visited the Hector Pierson museum, no photography allowed because the walls are covered with scenes from the massacre of twelve-year old Hector and hundreds of others in nineteen seventy-six for refusing to use textbooks written in Afrikaans. We ate lunch under one of the two huge cooling towers of a defunct power station, entirely covered in murals, with a bungee jumping apparatus strung between them.

I could not have packed more into that month and I am still sorting through my photos and videos, nor could I have done it all without Michael and Janet's help and hospitality. I understand now that my brother was really powerless to stay involved in the lives of Jackie and his two children, but he had gone on to make a good life for his new family and they all clearly have warm relations and good careers and a great appreciation for the awesome nature that surrounds them. Michael made a success of his life, runs cross-country races to stay fit, and keeps a fine wine cellar. Long may it last.

Since you are reading this it is self-evident that my moribund writing career is resurrected, but what of my original writing project? Whatever the merits of the story or the writing itself it has always suffered from the fact that at a hundred and forty thousand words, about four hundred and fifty pages, it would be too big a risk for any Irish publisher and major publishers elsewhere would not take the time to evaluate a long novel based on a mostly unknown mythology peppered with hard to pronounce names and Irish words. In the world of conventional publishing it was always doomed never to see the light of day.

But we no longer live in that world of manuscripts and galleys and seasonal publishing calendars and book tours, or at least there is now an alternative one. Earlier in twenty twenty-two I attended a Stanford course on self-publishing and that set me on a new path. I would launch *The Ulstermen* directly on Amazon Kindle Direct Publishing. The only real out of pocket cost for me was the cover design. And there it is in both ebook and on demand paperback version, and I will have done the same with this memoir, *Out Of Step,* by the time you read this. No-one needs to invest in an economic print run because this is print on demand. There is no publishing deadline that must coincide with the book's publicity and maybe it will or won't take on a life of its own. We shall see, but these stories are not now confined to some musty shelf, becoming mildewed if it is damp enough, or crumbling to dust if the paper dries out. They are digital files that, short of Armageddon, will be around forever. And I have many more stories in me the telling of which will fill my days for whatever compos mentis years are left to me.

My final closing thought is, of course, would my life have taken some other course had my sister not told all these lies? If my mother had had a caring supportive daughter next to her on that beach in Spain would she have still needed me to come home? If I had not been so hell-bent on not being like my father, would I have spent all those years writing or would I have stuck with my career in industry? Would I have married Kate? Would I have Justin and Helen? It's not that I yearn for all those might-have-beens, nor do I believe in parallel universes where some other version of me exists. What would Frida Kahlo have done if her spine had not been shattered in that tram crash in Mexico City? Are we all just ants on a log with no control over our destiny?

We now know that most stars are solar systems with planets and moons revolving around the stars. We know that these are formed from the protoplanetary disk that spins around the star when it is first born. There are so many of these that we know we will eventually find planets similar to earth and so a debate rages in the world of astrobiology as to whether it is inevitable or impossible that we will find beings similar to ourselves. If we rewound the evolutionary clock here on earth, would the world today be unrecognizable or the same? The divergent school says one answer and the convergent school another. A bat and a swallow do the same thing - they both evolved to fly through the air and catch insects - yet one is a furry mammal and the other is a feathered dinosaur.

I lean to the convergence. After all, by the time I stood on that beach in Spain on that fateful day, my formative years were behind me. I was a man in full, already conflicted, with both a technical career and an artistic avocation. Though I was railroaded into engineering school, I always had a love of literature and had written poetry as a teenager. Academically I was a good all-rounder, but English was the one subject that I was not physically punished for along the way. Writing was in my blood just as music and art are in the blood of others, and conflict is the life-blood of storytelling. Thanks for your time and more to come.

END

Acknowledgements

I am enormously grateful to those who read my first draft and I list them here in no particular order. My son and daughter, Justin and Helen, both of my ex-wives, Kate Kenny and Peg Fordney, my brothers Michael and Finbarr, my cousin Robert Kenny and my old friends Bill Corr and Michael Finegan all fed me thoughts and encouragement. John Harney, who is my sister Mary's ex-husband, both of whom feature prominently in this book, was unstinting in his help and inputs as was his wife, Janet Dwyer, who patiently proof-read the entire manuscript. My beloved uncle Tony passed away before I completed this but I know he knew before the end that I have finally set the record straight.

I should also acknowledge a long list of mentors and catalysts who drove or accompanied me on the zig-zag course of my life. There were my aunts, Ena Skally and Hilary Dunphy, the Nolan family, and the various business colleagues, John Sheehan, Richard Box, Guy Forney, Dan MacLoughlin, Joe O'Sullivan, Miriam Poland and then the writing-life inspirers and guides, Maureen Donegan, Garrett O'Connor, Fionnula Flanagan, Seamus Cashman, Ciara Considine, Steve Goldsmith, Tom Hayden, Patricia Monaghan, and many more who helped me to stay in step, or out of step, depending on your point of view.

Finally there is that personal inner library of writers of better books than mine, and of plays and songs and movies, and visual artists who tell their stories with brush or camera. This is where those of us who dream of being professional dreamers often glean our best ideas.